REMEMBER THE SABBATH DAY

IS THE LORD'S DAY STILL RELEVANT IN THE TWENTY-FIRST CENTURY?

Lewis Branch of Day One / LDOS

DayOne

ISBN 978-1-84625-719-3

British Library Cataloguing in Publication Data available

Lewis Branch of Day One / LDOS

Day One Publications
Ryelands Road, Leominster, HR6 8NZ, England
Tel 01568 613 740
North America Toll Free 888 329 6630
email sales@dayone.co.uk
web www.dayone.co.uk

The image on the cover is used under licence from Shutterstock.com

Printed by 4edge Limited

Contents

Introduction 5

Chapter 1: A Day to Remember 8

Chapter 2: A Day to Observe 20

Chapter 3: A Day to Rest 38

Chapter 4: A Day to Believe 49

Chapter 5: A Day to Worship 67

Chapter 6: A Day to Hope 85

Chapter 7: Conclusion 100

Introduction

Introduction

Rev. George MacAskill

Rev. George MacAskill, is the retired minister of the Stornoway congregation of the Associated Presbyterian Churches

Is 'The Lord's Day' still relevant in the twenty-first century? Everybody knows that Christianity has something to do with the Ten Commandments. But are there only nine commandments nowadays? Is there one that is no longer required? God's Law proceeds from God's nature. God's nature is unchangeable, so His laws are unchangeable. God's laws are immune from cultural change, political correctness and paradigm shifts in opinion. Religion is a matter of truth not preference, and truth is truth whether we believe it or not. Something does not *become* true simply because we believe it strongly enough. If I put my finger in the fire it will get burnt whether I believe it will or not. I will be diagnosed with cancer according to the biopsy result, not according to what I feel or believe. Religion is *following* God's own instructions about how to worship Him. Religion is not a matter of choice or popularity, but a case of what is right. We keep the commandments, not because they are convenient or fashionable, but because they are authentic.

The Fourth Commandment to 'keep the Sabbath Day' is not an 'optional extra' for enthusiasts—it was there between the Third Commandment and the Fifth Commandment from the moment God engraved them on tablets of stone.

It is also vitally important for Christians to grasp that the Law of God is for all nations and all times. It is not a temporary Jewish thing for Israel alone. This is demonstrated by the fact that the theological *basis* for giving the Fourth Commandment is the creation ordinance recorded in Exodus 20:11: 'For in six days the LORD made the heavens and the earth, the sea, and all that is in them, and rested the seventh day. *Therefore* the

LORD blessed the Sabbath Day, and hallowed it.' The Sabbath is based on creation and existed even before the Fall of Man. The Law of God must have been known by the people before they received it from God on Mount Sinai, as recorded in Exodus 20. This is confirmed in Exodus 16:28: 'How long refuse ye to keep my commandments and my laws?'

We also need to remember that one purpose of the Fourth Commandment is that it would serve as a lasting *sign* of God's people. 'Speak thou also unto the children of Israel, saying, Verily my sabbaths ye shall keep: for it is a sign between me and you throughout your generations; that ye may know that I am the LORD that doth sanctify you' (Exodus 31:13). The word translated 'sign' is translated elsewhere in the Bible as 'token' and 'mark'. Exodus 16:4 categorically states that the Sabbath is used as a test of allegiance to God: 'Then said the LORD unto Moses, Behold, I will rain bread from heaven for you; and the people shall go out and gather a certain rate every day, *that I may prove them, whether they will walk in my law, or no*.' Perhaps it could be inferred that the Church now lives in an age of relative insecurity, uncertainty and confusion precisely because we often sit loose to the promise implied in this commandment.

Those who think that the Fourth Commandment is no longer in force in **New Testament times** need to explain why Christ did not say so when He healed the man at the Pool of Bethesda (John 5) and the man born blind (John 9). When charged with breaking the Sabbath, did he not have an opportunity to demonstrate that the Fourth Commandment was no longer in force?

Deuteronomy 5:15 is a very enlightening verse. In that chapter the Bible is recording the Ten Commandments for the second time. Verse 15 reads: 'And remember that thou wast a servant in the land of Egypt, and that the LORD thy God brought thee out of thence through a mighty hand and by a stretched out arm: *therefore* the Lord thy God commanded thee to keep the sabbath day.' Here we are given the reason Christians are to keep the commandments of God. Many think that the Israelites were to keep the commandments so that they would *get into* the promised land—but, no, the reason believers are to keep the commandments is *gratitude to God* for already delivering them from bondage. In the first reading of the Ten

Commandments this reason is given in the first few verses of Exodus 20, which is often called the Preface to the Ten Commandments. Here, in the second reading of the Law in Deuteronomy 5, it is given after which commandment? None other than the Fourth commandment! Very strange if it was afterwards to be left out!

If you have difficulty appreciating the necessity of Sabbath observance in the New Testament era, you should find this book very helpful. There is much in it that addresses the issue of its necessity and benefit; of clarity regarding what is required of us on this day; and how best we can enjoy the day and benefit from adhering to its claims.

We trust that you will find faithfulness to Scripture, personal strength, support and blessing in these pages.

Chapter 1: A Day to Remember

Rev. Stephen McCollum

Rev. Stephen McCollum is the minister of Airdrie Reformed Presbyterian Church (formerly of Stornoway Reformed Presbyterian Church)

In the history of the human race, there has never been a week without a Sabbath. That is an incredible thought! God created Adam and Eve on the sixth day to be the pinnacle of His creation. They slept that night and awoke to the sunshine of the first Sabbath day. The Fall, which plunged our first parents into sin and misery, did not rob them of this weekly event, even when they had to leave Paradise. In all the subsequent years of human history the weekly Sabbath has continued, and if, by God's grace, you are spared to reach the current average life expectancy you will experience over 4,200 Sabbath days in your lifetime. But as week gives way to week this special day can become mundane or undervalued if we are not careful. I wonder if you feel that the day has become less special. It is essential that we begin this book by remembering why the day exists in the first place.

1. Remember that God has created

The weekly Sabbath is not something that has developed over time whether as a matter of expediency or through the dominance of any one culture. Rather, its inception is as ancient as the world itself. Moreover, the very concept of a week, which is well established worldwide, can be traced to the same origin.

Various governments have experimented with adjusting the length of a week, although invariably they have failed to make their changes endure. For example, the USSR instituted a five-day week in 1929. Each year had seventy-two 'weeks' plus five national holidays. This endeavour was used to try to increase industrial production. Each Russian worker worked four shifts out of five, but not every worker had the same day off. Therefore, the factories were continuously running, just with a different rotation of staff. The venture failed and the USSR reverted to the seven-day week. In fact, in some rural areas the seven-day week was maintained throughout the unsuccessful initiative.

But why do we have seven days per week rather than, say, ten days? Why is it that a five-day week is doomed to fail? Is there a scientific basis for the week? For instance, we know that a year is when the earth orbits the sun once. Is the length of a week related to astronomy, perhaps following the lunar cycle? Although it takes approximately four weeks to move through all the phases of the moon, it is not exactly so. Bear in mind that a full moon does not occur on the same day of the week each month. The week is not an astronomically-determined measurement but rather, as the Bible shows, it is a God-instituted unit of time given to humanity in Eden. Any attempts to erase the week are attempts to erase the Creator.

The first Sabbath

> Thus the heavens and the earth, and all the host of them, were finished. And on the seventh day God ended His work which He had done, and He rested on the seventh day from all His work which He had done. Then God blessed the seventh day and sanctified it, because in it He rested from all His work which God had created and made (Genesis 2:1–3).

Perhaps Adam and Eve woke on that seventh day anticipating further acts of creation, some new marvels. The Godhead (Father, Son, and Holy Spirit) had finished making the heavens and the earth. This seventh day broke the literary rhythm established in Genesis 1. When we read that chapter, we hear repetition: 'Then God said … God called … and God saw that it was good … So the evening and the morning…'. Yet this pattern does not continue further than six days. On the seventh day, the Creator made nothing new, but rather rested and gave honour to the day itself. In the verses that start the second chapter four key verbs are used to show what God's activity was in that day. These verbs may be considered in two pairs: ended and rested; blessed and sanctified.

God ended His work and rested

> And on the seventh day God ended His work which He had done, and He rested on the seventh day from all His work which He had done (Genesis 2:2).

God's work of creation was completed on the sixth day when He made Adam and Eve. The seventh day was marked by accomplishment—everything was done; God's creative work was finished. When the Creator looked at the universe, He saw nothing lacking but was satisfied by what He had constructed. Therefore, He rested. It is hard for us to imagine the perfection of this world. When we make a piece of art, no matter what medium it is in, we often find ourselves seeing its imperfections. We could almost continue forever making an adjustment here or there to get it just so. But the Master Artist stopped. The entirety of what He had made, each brushstroke, was very good (Genesis 1:31).

God's cessation from further creation is called rest. When we consider the idea of rest, we automatically associate it with weariness and exhaustion. After a day at work, we come home drained and needing rest. However, the almighty God had not expended Himself in creating all things. The omnipotent One was not tired from six days of work. He does not slumber or sleep (Psalm 121:4) because He does not need it. Consider Isaiah's words,

> Have you not known? Have you not heard? The everlasting God, the LORD, the Creator of the ends of the earth, neither faints nor is weary. His understanding is unsearchable (Isaiah 40:28).

In fact, this passage in Isaiah goes on to demonstrate that, far from God lacking energy, He is the one who renews the strength of the weary.

The Lord did not rest on the seventh day because He needed to recuperate. Nor was this resting complete idleness or inactivity. Our

Maker continues to hold together the universe daily, governing all affairs wisely. The Creator had finished creating, but He must still providentially rule over His creation. This work will never stop.

God's 'rest' on the seventh day was abstaining from further creative work and thus exemplary, setting the pattern for mankind to rest on one day in seven. In fact, the Hebrew words for 'rest' and 'Sabbath' are related. Six days of every week are engaged in toil. Each Lord's Day we have Divine permission and blessing to take a break, both from the uncompleted tasks of the week before and from the anxious thoughts about pressing duties in the week ahead.

Isn't this weekly pause highly desirable for tired bodies, minds, and souls? The modern working environment is stressful. There may be heavy expectations from employers, such as long hours, high standards, and tight deadlines. Add to these things the burdens of family life, the countless tasks on the to-do list. Perhaps the best remedy is staring us in the face—the work week needs a 'weekend', or more precisely (as will be seen in a later chapter) a fresh start with the right priorities. I wonder how much more productive we would be if we all followed the Divine example? Would there not be greater well-being in the work environment because of it?

God blessed the day and sanctified it

> Then God blessed the seventh day and sanctified it, because in it He rested from all His work which God had created and made (Genesis 2:3).

The first Sabbath day was not merely marked by what God did not do. We see that He both blessed and sanctified the day. God had already blessed the birds and fish that they might multiply (Genesis 1:22), and humans created in His image that they might 'be fruitful and multiply; fill the earth and subdue it; have dominion over the fish of the sea, over the birds of the air, and over every living thing that moves on the earth' (Genesis 1:28). Now God blesses something inanimate—a day. Thus God gave the Sabbath a purpose and fruitfulness. The Sabbath was made for the blessing of man (Mark 2:27) in a way that no other day would be.

We can go further and say that the Sabbath was to bring holy blessings for man. There are many physical and temporal blessings that God gives (Psalm 145:15–16) and we ought to look to Him alone for those provisions. Each day we pray for our daily bread (Matthew 6:11). But the blessings of the weekly special Day go further. Not only did God bless the Sabbath day, He also sanctified it.

When something was sanctified, it was dedicated to a religious purpose, distinct from other things. The word 'sanctified' is used throughout the Old Testament for people and things set apart for God, particularly for the worship of the Eternal One. Everything about the Israelites' worship was to be distinct and holy, according to the Divine pattern. So too, the weekly Sabbath was set aside by God. He did not merely sanctify the first Sabbath day, but the Sabbath as an institution. It is distinct from the six common days of work and is the true pinnacle of the week. As God is holy, so His day is to be holy and, as is revealed later, His people are to be holy: 'Surely My Sabbaths you shall keep, for it is a sign between Me and you throughout your generations, that you may know that I am the LORD who sanctifies you' (Exodus 31:13).

I wonder whether you have experienced the holy blessings that God gives uniquely on His Day. Perhaps the Lord's Day at times becomes mundane because we forget to seek a blessing, or more particularly that we fail to seek the One who blesses (Hebrews 11:6). Just as those who would come near God must regard Him as holy (Leviticus 10:3), so those who would worship Him on the Sabbath must regard the whole day as holy (Exodus 20:8). Consider Isaiah's words, particularly how if we keep the holiness and honour of the Sabbath we may expect blessings:

> If you turn away your foot from the Sabbath,
> From doing your pleasure on My holy day,
> And call the Sabbath a delight,
> The holy day of the Lord honourable,
> And shall honour Him, not doing your own ways,
> Nor finding your own pleasure,
> Nor speaking your own words,

> Then you shall delight yourself in the LORD;
> And I will cause you to ride on the high hills of the earth,
> And feed you with the heritage of Jacob your father.
> The mouth of the LORD has spoken
>
> (Isaiah 58:13–14).

God's pattern followed in early history

Sometimes people argue that Sabbaths were a Jewish institution which began at Mount Sinai, particularly since the word 'Sabbath' does not appear in Genesis, and so there can be no evidence of Sabbath keeping. Arguments from silence are never convincing. Consider the logical conclusion of this reasoning. If the Sabbath is only a Jewish institution, originating as part of the laws binding the Old Testament people, it cannot be imposed on New Testament Christians. This chapter cannot deal with this faulty theological argument or with the relationship between the Old and New Testaments; however, let us see that we have reason to believe that what God did on the first Sabbath was observed in early history.

As we have seen, God gave the day special honour when only Adam and Eve existed. Nevertheless, in them, the whole human race stood before Him. All of humanity noticed what He had implemented. God's intention was that the day would be universally sanctified by Adam and Eve's descendants and that the regular pattern of seven-day weeks would continue throughout time.

The Bible shows that the concept of seven-day weeks was accepted from the earliest period of human history. When Noah was checking how much the waters had receded, he sent out a dove. The dove returned because there was nowhere to rest.

> And he waited yet another seven days, and again he sent the dove out from the ark. Then the dove came to him in the evening, and behold, a freshly plucked olive leaf was in her mouth; and Noah knew that the waters had receded from the earth. So he waited yet another seven days and sent out the dove, which did not return again to him anymore (Genesis 8:10–12).

We can see that the waiting period Noah chose is marked by two measurements of seven days, or two weeks. I doubt that the intervals were inadvertent or random. May we not infer that Noah was familiar with a seven-day week?

Furthermore, when Jacob was tricked into marrying Leah by his uncle Laban we read,

> And Laban said, 'It must not be done so in our country, to give the younger before the firstborn. Fulfil her week, and we will give you this one also for the service which you will serve with me still another seven years.' Then Jacob did so and fulfilled her week. So he gave him his daughter Rachel as wife also (Genesis 29:26–28).

The idea of a week was well known to Laban in Mesopotamia, so much so that marriage feasts were week-long activities. The God-ordained pattern of weeks was being followed in early history.

Even when we turn to the Sabbath law at Mount Sinai, we should not suspect that Jehovah's people did not observe Sabbaths already. In fact, we have reason to believe that they did already understand that they were to mark the Sabbath weekly. This point is demonstrated in the reason that reinforces the Fourth Commandment.

> Remember the Sabbath day, to keep it holy. Six days you shall labour and do all your work, but the seventh day is the Sabbath of the LORD your God. In it you shall do no work: you, nor your son, nor your daughter, nor your male servant, nor your female servant, nor your cattle, nor your stranger who is within your gates. For in six days the LORD made the heavens and the earth, the sea, and all that is in them, and rested the seventh day. Therefore the LORD blessed the Sabbath day and hallowed it (Exodus 20:8–11).

By stating the command in the way He did, the Lawgiver presupposed a knowledge of the Sabbath concept. He was not making a new ceremony that was outside the Hebrews' experience. Not only did they understand the principle of dedicating time to their God, something that all religions do to some degree, but more particularly the weekly pattern of six days followed by one day was well-ingrained. God had also already instructed them about not collecting manna on the Sabbath (Exodus 16:23).

It was reasonable for their Master to enjoin Sabbath observance, not least because He practised it Himself first. We can go further and say that all of humanity ought to set apart Sabbaths for this very reason. The origins of the day of rest were not in Jewish law. We may in fact call the Sabbath a creation ordinance, that is, a command given by God before the Fall, which is binding on every person, in every culture, throughout every age. The Sabbath reminds us of creation.

2. Remember that God has saved

Nevertheless, as we think about why the Sabbath day exists at all, it would be wrong to think only of God's work of creation. Indeed, even in the giving of the Law, God gives two separate things to remember about this special day. We should keep the Sabbath day holy:

> For in six days the LORD made the heavens and the earth, the sea, and all that is in them, and rested the seventh day. Therefore the LORD blessed the Sabbath day and hallowed it (Exodus 20:11).

> And remember that you were a slave in the land of Egypt, and the LORD your God brought you out from there by a mighty hand and by an outstretched arm; therefore the LORD your God commanded you to keep the Sabbath day (Deuteronomy 5:15).

Taking this second reason it is evident that the Sabbath day is also a day to remember salvation. For the Hebrews they could remember back to a period of slavery, of hard and torturous bondage. Their gracious covenant God had redeemed them and so the Sabbath day became a time to celebrate that redemption afresh. In the six working days of each week the Israelite might have been focused on the daily tasks of his farm or trade. Each Sabbath was a call to remember that the Israelites had been freed by the Almighty's hand. The weekly Sabbath helped them to do so. They must never forget it.

The Old Testament uses the Exodus as one of the major pictures of salvation. It is referenced and alluded to very often, pointing us forward to redemption in Christ, our Passover lamb (1 Corinthians 5:7). There is no way to be relieved from the guilt of sin without sacrifice, for 'without shedding of blood there is no remission' of sins (Hebrews 9:22). But the blood of Jesus, this 'blood of the new covenant ... is shed for many for the remission of sins' (Matthew 26:28). What a blessed hope we have through a loving Saviour! Christ, the sinless substitute, has purchased every spiritual blessing for His people.

The Christian is to remember with gratitude his salvation regularly. But how easy it is to become engrossed in the temporal matters of the six days, with job responsibilities. Our occupations literally occupy our minds. When each Sabbath day comes the Christian's priorities are recalibrated. Did he forget his redemption? Did his Saviour feature in his thoughts? On the Sabbath we get our minds reset as we are renewed in the blessings of the covenant.

Just as the Old Testament cloud of witnesses kept the Sabbath, so too New Testament saints are to remember their salvation on the weekly Sabbath, or Lord's Day. Monumentally the day has changed from Saturday to Sunday (as will be considered in a later chapter), although this change gives prominence to the power of Christ's resurrection. What a glorious truth to consider not merely once a year but on each Lord's Day!

The weekly Sabbath does not only remind Christians of their salvation, but it also proclaims the glorious gospel of Christ to a fallen world. Do we want to see more conversions? In order to win over the world, we ought not to become like them in how they despise the weekly Sabbath. Rather the Lord's Day offers hope to a world sunk in the bog of sin and misery. It is a day when Christ is offered freely to all. As Christ has made us new, he can do the same for others. The Lord's Day is a day for angels to rejoice in heaven over sinners brought to repentance.

Having said that, what happens if the church loses its Sabbaths through carelessness and neglect? Not only will there be less focus on redemption, but the watching world will not regard the gospel as serious. Let me give you an example. Imagine that someone says to you that they want to become a concert pianist and yet you know that they do not spend time practising. You would conclude that they were not very dedicated to their goal because they did not put in the time. We give time to what we are serious about; we devote time to the people we love. That is why analysing how we spend our time is one way to test if we have any idols in our hearts. When Christians set apart a seventh part of their lives to rejoice in the gospel of Christ, a watching world will recognise them as serious about Christ. When they ask us why our Sundays are not like theirs, we have the perfect opportunity to speak of redemption.

3. Remember that humans have souls

The Sabbath calls on us to remember the past events of creation and redemption. But there is a remarkable opportunity on the day to remember that we have never-dying souls. Our Maker did not form humans as simply flesh and blood. We have a spiritual dimension too and our souls are made for eternity. The Lord's Day helps us to look forward as well as back.

Hebrews 4 explores the theme of rest and will be considered more thoroughly elsewhere in this book. Nevertheless, let us note that it examines what the Sabbath prefigures. Both the first Sabbath after creation (Hebrews 4:4) and the redeemed people entering their rest in the promised land of Canaan (4:8) point forward. 'There remains therefore a rest for the people of God' (4:9). Every Sabbath helps prepare the saints for eternity in heaven.

Have you ever come to the end of a blessed Lord's day? Perhaps the sermon particularly spoke to you, the singing was heavenly, and the fellowship was sweet. Did you wish that the day could continue forever? This longing is just what we should feel because the Sabbath looks forward to the everlasting Sabbath.

The Puritans sometimes called the Lord's Day the 'market day of the soul' and this designation is a helpful illustration of the potential each Lord's Day holds. Imagine a world without shops open twenty-four hours a day. Imagine a world where the town's market day was the only opportunity to buy certain foods or household goods. Before going to market you would make a plan—what will you need to buy and how much? Perhaps you would write a list to ensure you get all that you need. But once you had been to the market and the stalls were packed away, there would be no opportunity to go back to pick up a few extras. If you forgot something from your list, you would have to make-do until the next week's market day. The market day was a day of business and trade and, in social terms, a high point of the week.

So too, for the Christian, the Lord's Day is the pinnacle of the week. We must not view it as a day we may squander in idleness. Instead, it is a day to prepare for and use wisely. We have business to transact with God on this day. It is a day for abiding in Christ, our risen Saviour, communing with Him in His Word and prayer, and as we do so we will bear much fruit (John 15:5). It is a day for gathering with Christ's people to worship the Triune God and fellowship together in order that we are stirred up to good works (Hebrews 10:24–25). It is a day for spiritual purposes.

It is worth contemplating how much more zealous Christians would be if they made use of this 'market day of the soul'. We would be more fruitful if our fellowship with the Triune God was richer, deeper, and more frequent. Perhaps we lament not having much time in our busy schedules. The Lord's Day takes away that excuse, if we use it wisely. Instead of reckoning it as a day of drudgery to be endured, we ought to be receptive to the manifold opportunity the day presents for growth in grace.

When the people of Israel were traversing the wilderness God provided them with times of refreshing from the arduous journey. One such place was Elim 'where there were twelve wells of water and seventy palm trees' (Exodus 15:27). The Israelites camped there next to the source of water. Is that not the way we should view the Lord's Day? As pilgrims travelling to Immanuel's Land, we recognise that the way is not easy. When God provides weekly spiritual refreshment for the journey let us be sure to make the most of it. Our souls need the Lord's Day more than we may think.

Conclusion

The Lord's Day can become mundane if we are not careful to remember its wonderful origins and purpose. Many Christians have settled for the Sabbath to become a second Saturday. Some churches offer Saturday services so that attendees can have their Sundays free. Perhaps for you, the Sabbath is not special now. I wonder if your life is hectic, lacking in balance. Are you part of the fast-paced 24/7 lifestyle? Have you forgotten that God has given a day of rest? The Sabbath reminds us of creation, that the day is set apart from the other six days of the week. It prompts us to remember salvation through the Lord Jesus Christ. It ensures that we do not forget the needs of our souls.

I began this chapter noting that the Sabbath institution, which began in Eden, has continued throughout human history and that those who live to old age will experience thousands of Lord's Days in their lifetimes. I wonder how many you have experienced. I wonder how many you have left unused. Be sure to remember the reason why the day exists at all.

Ev'n as with marrow and with fat
my soul shall fillèd be;
Then shall my mouth with joyful lips
sing praises unto thee:

When I do thee upon my bed
remember with delight,
And when on thee I meditate
in watches of the night.

(Psalm 63:5–6)

Chapter 2: A Day to Observe

Rev. Paul Murray

Rev. Paul Murray is the minister of the Kinloch congregation of the Free Church of Scotland

Introduction

The benefits of having one day in seven set aside for rest and worship are, from a Christian perspective, difficult to deny. As well as easily identifying the primary day on which the Church should gather for worship, it provides the Christian with a day to devote to 'growth in grace and in the knowledge of our Lord and Saviour Jesus Christ' (2 Peter 3:18). In this respect, the observance of the Lord's Day has long been held to be indispensable for both a healthy Christian and a healthy church. As Thomas Boston explains:

> God is in a special manner concerned for the keeping of the Sabbath, it being that on which all religion depends. Accordingly, as it is observed or disregarded, so it readily goes with the other parts of religion.[1]

What Boston is saying is that if Sabbath observance is not part of our lives, our Christianity will be disjointed and incomplete. The Sabbath is the mortar which binds the Christian life together. The position of the Fourth Commandment within the structure of the Ten, being a bridge between the God-facing commandments (1–3) and the man-facing commandments (5–10), points us to its central importance. It has rightly been called the keystone commandment in that the others depend on it for their own proper fulfilment. In this context, James Durham wrote:

1 Thomas Boston, *The Complete Works of Thomas Boston*, Vol. 2, Ed., Samuel Macmillan, Stoke-on-Trent: Tentmaker Publications, 2002, p. 187.

> This command is placed in a manner between the two tables, because it is a transition as it were from the one to the other, and contains in it duties of immediate service to God, and of charity towards men, and so in some sort serves to reconcile (if we may speak so) the two tables, and to knit them together, that so their harmony may be the more clearly seen.[2]

As such, it is difficult to overstate how beneficial it is for the Christian to have a Sabbath that can be dedicated to God. In God's wise creation order, He has given six days for man to make a living, provide for a family, and fulfil all his other responsibilities, knowing that these six days are necessary for his physical prosperity. Likewise, He has given one day out of seven that is to be cordoned specifically for the things of God. The inescapable logic is that He has given this day because man needs it for his spiritual prosperity.[3] In this light, the Sabbath ought to be viewed as a very precious gift.

As beneficial as Sabbath observance may be, however, it must be based on more than just the fact that it is beneficial. Otherwise, despite its many benefits, it becomes a matter of choice rather than a matter of obligation.[4] The view which this book upholds is that Sabbath observance is not a matter of personal preference but one of Christian obedience. This chapter will seek to prove its ongoing legitimacy on account of its inclusion in the perpetually relevant Ten Commandments.

Under authority?

Before we come to the Ten Commandments, however, it is important that we grasp the concept of authority in the Christian life more generally. In our increasingly individualistic and subjectivist culture, authority is constantly

---

2 James Durham, *Practical Exposition of The Ten Commandments*, Dallas: Naphtali Press, 2002, p. 205.

3 For a more detailed argument along these lines, see Terry L. Johnson, *Christian Growth and the 'Missing Link'*, in The Banner of Truth Magazine, August & September 2020, Edinburgh: Banner of Truth, pp. 50–51.

4 For example, a minister could advise his congregation to read through the Bible in a year, knowing that this would be helpful for them. However, if God does not prescribe such a course, it must remain a recommendation rather than a command.

under attack in both society at large and the Church specifically. At the end of the nineteenth century, the Dutch theologian Herman Bavinck could write that,

> There are many people in our time who reject every idea of sovereignty in the family, the state, and society and want nothing to do with anything other than democracy and anarchy. Under the influence of this view there are also those who in theology find the idea of God as king too reminiscent of the Old Testament and antiquated...[5]

This rejection of authority[6] has continued apace since Bavinck's day as traditional structures of authority have collapsed, one by one. Sadly, even many evangelical churches have been unable, or unwilling, to stem the anti-authoritarian tide. As unqualified obedience to authority in the form of parents, employers, or church courts becomes a relic of the past, it is no surprise that unqualified obedience to God and His Word on the part of the Christian, whether explicit or implicit, is likewise under attack. As such, it is not uncommon for people to be willing to take Christ as a loving Saviour to forgive them, but not as an authoritative Lord to reign over the details of their lives.

As cultures change and as views on authority vary over time, the Bible unashamedly retains its position that man is to 'Render ... to all their dues: tribute to whom tribute is due; custom to whom custom; fear to whom fear; honour to whom honour' (Romans 13:7). The immediate context in Romans 13 is that a government ought to be obeyed within its own jurisdiction, but the underlying principle, being that of the Fifth Commandment, extends beyond that to obedience to all lawful authority, including parents (Ephesians 6:1), employers (Ephesians 6:5) and church courts (Matthew 28:18–20; Ephesians 4:11–12; Acts 20:28).

---

5 Herman Bavinck, *Reformed Dogmatics*, Vol. 2., translated by John Vriend, edited by John Bolt, Grand Rapids: Baker Publishing Group, 2004, p. 615.

6 The notable exception to this trajectory is in the case of a democratically elected human government where, arguably, the opposite is the case.

Its supreme reference, however, is that of man being under the authority of God. As creatures of this Creator, and subjects of this King, all of mankind is answerable to Him and owe Him their obedience. For such obedience to have any tangible reality, however, it must be measured by law. That law, found in Scripture, is normally referred to as the moral law.

Natural law

The origin of the moral law is central to any argument for its continued relevance. The moral law is, essentially, a reflection of God's own character and morality. For this very reason, God delights in its proper observance (Jeremiah 9:24). Because man is made in God's image (Genesis 1:27), in his sinless condition, he reflects this same character and morality. Explaining this, Francis Nigel Lee writes:

> The moral law has its ontical and historical source in God, the absolute GOOD. Historically, God next embodied His moral law in the inward conscience of His image, namely unfallen man, writing it on the tables of his heart.[7]

For this reason, the Westminster Shorter Catechism speaks of man being created 'in knowledge, righteousness and holiness'.[8] These three qualities have no substance unless they are defined by law. It is only reasonable to assume, then, that Adam knew the moral law, not because he had it written in a book or on tablets of stone, but because it was written upon his natural conscience. In the fearful and wonderful design of God, the essence of the Law, if not the letter, was made intrinsic to him; a part of the first man's psychological make-up.

When Adam sinned, the image of God in him and in his posterity was significantly marred so that obedience to the natural law was no longer the default position. However, God's image in man was not completely removed (1 Corinthians 11:7; James 3:9), so there continued to be an innate, although imperfect, understanding of what God required of him.

7 Francis Nigel Lee, *The Covenantal Sabbath*, London: Lord's Day Observance Society, 1966, p. 23.
8 Westminster Shorter Catechism, Question 10.

Failure to act in accordance with this knowledge is the essence of sin. As Bavinck explains:

> Sin, which entered the world as a result of Adam's trespass, was also present and dominant in the time from Adam to Moses, when God had not yet announced his law; then, too, people sinned ... death reigned from Adam to Moses, even though at the time people did not transgress any concrete, explicitly announced divine law and could therefore not sin in the likeness of Adam's trespass. Still, they sinned because they too had a law then that was known to them 'by nature' (Romans 1:18ff.; 2:12–15). After all, if death reigned then, sin must also have reigned then.[9]

As such, Paul can speak about the heathen people in his own day having 'the work of the law written in their hearts, their conscience also bearing witness' (Romans 2:15). This is why those who sin, even without having ever heard the Ten Commandments read, are still guilty of their sin—because God has given each man the natural law through their conscience. This, too, explains how, in committing sin and idolatry, the heathen know 'the judgment of God, that they which commit such things are worthy of death' (Romans 1:32).

If God's moral law is natural, you would expect to see traces of it between Adam's creation and the formal announcement of it in Exodus 20. Such expectations are not disappointed. Cain's killing of his brother was still treated as murder, thousands of years before 'thou shalt not kill' was ever inscribed on the tablets of stone. Likewise, Abimelech understood that a relationship with Sarah, Abraham's wife, would be adultery (Genesis 20:9), and Rachel's taking of her father's idols was understood to be both stealing and idolatry (Genesis 31:19)—and this all before the law was formally delivered at Sinai.

Neither is the Sabbath commandment absent in this period. From the time of its ordinance at creation (Genesis 2:2–3), through to it being

9 Herman Bavinck, *Reformed Dogmatics*, Vol. 3., translated by John Vriend, edited by John Bolt, Grand Rapids: Baker Publishing Group, 2004, p. 84.

formally given at Sinai, there are numerous veiled allusions to it.[10] There is a clear reference to it in Exodus 16 where the children of Israel were told to gather twice as much manna on the sixth day of the week in order to observe the Sabbath (Exodus 16:22–30). The fact that this was required before the giving of the law proves that the Fourth Commandment was not an innovation but was already known to the people, although it had evidently fallen into abeyance. Lee cites Exodus 5:5 as evidence that one of the great burdens of Israel's Egyptian bondage was that they were unable to keep the Sabbath.[11]

Old Testament laws

At this point, it is important for us to understand the special place of the Ten Commandments among the many laws given to Old Testament Israel. It is certainly true that Christians are not obligated to keep every law given to Israel in the Old Testament. But why some and not others? In order to answer that question, we need to understand the different types of law in the Old Testament.

Theologians have traditionally classified the Old Testament laws into three different groups—ceremonial laws, civil laws, and moral laws. It is true that these classifications do not appear in Scripture and, for the unassuming Old Testament Jew, the Law would have just been the law. They were equally obliged to observe them all, regardless of classification. Nevertheless, these three categories are helpful to understand the evident differences between these laws and why some of them still apply today whereas others do not.[12]

Ceremonial law

The ceremonial or religious laws include details on the festivals and sacrifices which characterised Old Testament worship. These laws have

10 For a fascinating study of these allusions, see Francis Nigel Lee, *The Covenantal Sabbath*, pp. 83–148.

11 The word translated *'rest'* in most English translations is the root word from which *'Sabbath'* is taken.

12 For a thorough treatment of these classifications, see Philip S. Ross, *From the Finger of God*, Fearn: Christian Focus Publications, 2010.

to do with the specifically religious nature of Jewish life. Among other things, these laws give rules for the priesthood, sacrifices and ceremonies. They also include directions for the building of the tabernacle and the temple.

Clearly, for the Christian, these laws are fulfilled in the person and finished work of Jesus Christ. The Epistle to the Hebrews is largely taken up with this very topic—the fact that Jesus Christ is the fulfilment of, and is superior to, the Old Testament ceremonial law. For this reason, it would not just be out of place for Christians to offer sacrifices at their worship services—it would be sinful. Nevertheless, careful study of the ceremonial law will pay dividends for those who seek to gain a better picture of the God who, for a time, required them, and the Saviour who, in due time, fulfilled them.

Civil law

The civil laws were given to regulate daily life in Israel and were not unlike modern government legislation. They cover several topics and situations, including rules for restitution when a crime has been committed (Exodus 22:1), and laws pertaining to such subjects as food (Leviticus 11), hygiene (Deuteronomy 23:12–14), disease (Leviticus 13–15), health and safety (Deuteronomy 22:8), and a range of other diverse issues.[13]

With the passing away of the nation state of Israel, the civil law ceased to be applicable. That does not mean that both Church and state cannot learn from them today. They are outworkings of the moral law and, therefore, based on unchanging and perpetually relevant principles. In fact, a quick scan of the nation's statute book will show that most of these Old Testament civil laws have, in one form or another, been reinstated in our own country in the relatively recent past. God ensured that His people were well ahead of their time. The detail of these Israelite laws, however, are not binding upon the Christian today who is bound by the civil laws of his own nation.

---

13 See, for example, Deuteronomy 21:22-22:12. For a fuller description of Israel's civil laws, see Brian H Edwards, *The Ten Commandments for Today*, Epsom: Day One Publications, 2002, pp. 16–21.

The moral law

If the ceremonial law and the civil law are no longer directly applicable to the New Testament Christian, what makes the Ten Commandments different? In their substance, the Ten Commandments are the essence of the natural law which we have considered and are, therefore, a reflection of God's image. As such, these are not new laws but, rather, a concise summary of a universal law. As Boston explains, 'The commandment is exceeding broad, and runs through the whole Bible; but we have a summary or short view of it in the ten commands given by the Lord on Mount Sinai.'[14]

The unusual way in which the Ten Commandments were given highlights their importance. First, whereas the ceremonial and civil laws were given by God through Moses, the Ten Commandments were delivered directly by the voice of God (Exodus 20:1). Secondly, these laws were written down, not in the first place by scribes, but by the finger of God on two tables of stone (Deuteronomy 9:10). These two exceptional facts immediately indicate the importance of this law and point towards its permanence. Who, after all, can abolish what God has written with His own finger?

Another unique feature of the Ten Commandments is that the tablets on which they were written were placed in the Ark of the Covenant (Deuteronomy 10:2). The covenant of which the Ark was a symbol is the same covenant to which Christians belong—the covenant of grace. The Christian is, essentially, a New Testament Jew (Romans 2:28–29) and the Church of Christ is the continuation of Old Testament Israel (Romans 9:6; Galatians 6:16). It is only natural, then, that moral obedience in both Old and New Testaments should conform to the same law. In both dispensations, it is the Ten Commandments which defines what both righteousness and sin look like in God's eyes.[15]

---

14 Thomas Boston, *The Complete Works of Thomas Boston*, Vol. 2, p. 69.

15 It is for this reason that the evangelists were so careful to record Jesus' defences of Himself when accused of breaking the commandments. For Jesus to have truly broken the commandments would have given the Pharisees adequate proof that He was not the Messiah. For an example of this, see Matthew 12:1–14.

No longer under law?

Most evangelicals will concede that all men are born subject to God's authority and, therefore, under a law by which they shall be judged. They will not argue with the Westminster Larger Catechism which explains the moral law as being a 'declaration of the will of God to mankind, directing and binding everyone to personal, perfect, and perpetual conformity and obedience thereunto'.[16]

There are many, however, who argue that the Christian is no longer bound to keep the Law. Their central argument is that the Christian is released from obligation to the Law by virtue of their union with Christ through faith. They argue that Jesus Christ has fulfilled the Law in their place and, therefore, released them from its demands.[17]

A wider reading of Paul's argument, however, shows that he cannot possibly be suggesting that the Christian is no longer under law in that sense. In Romans 3:31 and elsewhere, he clearly denies making the Law void; on the contrary, he claims to be establishing it. Similarly, in the same context in which he speaks of becoming dead to the Law in Romans 7, he likewise describes 'the law [as] holy, and the commandment holy, and just, and good' (Romans 7:12). More than that, he can say that he 'delights in the law of God after the inward man' (Romans 7:22). Such language is very strange if Paul believes the moral law to be a thing of the past.

When Paul speaks of no longer being under the Law, he is clearly speaking about no longer being under its condemnation. After all, anyone who fails to perfectly keep the whole Law of God is under His wrath and curse (Galatians 3:10). However, the believer is made free from that curse because Jesus Christ has fulfilled the Law in his place and borne its curse in his stead (Galatians 3:13).

As such, Paul no longer sees himself as bound to keep the Law in order to save himself. Rather, as he treats this subject in more detail in Galatians 2 and 3, he can conclude that 'a man is not justified by the works of the law, but by the faith of Jesus Christ ... for by the works of the law shall no

16 Westminster Larger Catechism, Question 93.
17 Their arguments are often based on texts like Romans 6:14 and 7:4, 7.

flesh be justified' (Galatians 2:16; see also Romans 2:28). It is in this same sense that the believer, as Paul tells the Romans, is no longer 'under the law, but under grace' (Romans 6:15). He is not, therefore, saying that he is not under the law for obedience but, rather, that he is not under it for salvation.

Love vs law?

Another argument against the perpetuity of the moral law is that Christianity is not a religion governed by law, but a relationship governed by love. In support of this conclusion, those who hold to it cite the Apostle Paul who tells the Romans in chapter 13 that 'love is the fulfilling of the law' (Romans 13:10). Similarly, he explains to the Galatians that 'all the law is fulfilled in one word, even in this; Thou shalt love thy neighbour as thyself' (Galatians 5:14). It is argued that law-keeping, which is portrayed as a particular feature of Old Testament religion, is replaced by loving God and neighbour, which is portrayed as the particular feature of New Testament religion.

In answering this objection, it is important to recognise that there is a measure of truth in it. Christianity cannot be defined solely along the lines of religion and law-keeping. The Christian life includes that, but it is more than that—it is a loving relationship with God through Christ.

It is not, however, Biblical to pit either religion and relationship, or obedience and love—which are, in many ways, one and the same—against one another. On closer examination, both are clearly indispensable elements of the Christian life. The caricature of Old Testament religion being defined by law-keeping and New Testament religion by love simply does not stand up to Scriptural scrutiny.

For example, the Book of Deuteronomy—literally, the Second Law—has at its core the *Shema* of Deuteronomy 6:4–5: 'Hear, O Israel: The LORD our God is one LORD: And thou shalt love the LORD thy God with all thine heart, and with all thy soul, and with all thy might.' Numerous other instances could be cited, but this is sufficient proof that law and love clearly belonged together in Old Testament religious life.

Likewise, in the New Testament, the Apostle John, whose emphasis on the role of love in the Christian life is, arguably, stronger than any other,[18] is the same Apostle who defines that love in terms of law: 'For this is the love of God, that we keep his commandments: and his commandments are not grievous' (1 John 5:3). Again, this is proof that law and love belong together, and are powerless without one other, in the Christian life.[19]

The context of Romans 13, where Paul speaks of love being the fulfilment of the Law, is also important in this regard. Here, Paul calls those who live by love to 'walk properly, as in the day, not in revelry and drunkenness, not in lewdness and lust, not in strife and envy' (Romans 13:13). Love is, therefore, always governed by law. In any sphere of life, claiming to walk in love while living loose to the Law will inevitably lead to not walking in love at all.[20]

The Westminster Divines, often caricatured as legalists, were not blind to the central role of love in the Christian life. They clearly recognised it when they wrote that 'The sum of the Ten Commandments is, to love the Lord with all our heart, with all our soul, with all our strength, and with all our mind; and our neighbour as ourselves.'[21] They did not, however, understand love to be a substitute for the Ten Commandments but, rather, their totality. In other words, if you perfectly kept the Ten Commandments, you would simultaneously be loving God and your neighbour, and *vice versa*.

Jesus and the Law

To accept the continued relevance of the Ten Commandments for the Christian life today is the only way to explain the reverence with which Jesus Himself held the Ten Commandments. Not only did he recite them

18 In the King James Version of 1 John, John uses the word 'love' twenty-three times in five short chapters—more than any other New Testament book. In second place is John's Gospel, using it nineteen times, and in third place is Paul's Epistle to the Ephesians, using it fourteen times.

19 It is notable that the relationship between law and love is evident from common sense itself. If we are to love our neighbour or spouse or even our enemy, we need to know how we are to do that. If our love is lawless, it will inevitably end up being no love at all.

20 The same argument applies to walking in the Spirit (Gal. 5:16).

21 Westminster Shorter Catechism, Question 42.

to the rich young ruler in Mark 10, but He also spoke directly of their importance:

> Think not that I am come to destroy the law, or the prophets: I am not come to destroy, but to fulfil .... Whosoever therefore shall break one of these least commandments, and shall teach men so, he shall be called the least in the kingdom of heaven: but whosoever shall do and teach them, the same shall be called great in the kingdom of heaven (Matthew 5:17–19).

Clearly, for Jesus, fulfilment of the Law refers to more than His own observance of it and bearing of its curse. He is talking about commandments being practically taught and observed in the lives of His followers. This is evident from His subsequent challenge: 'For I say unto you, That except your righteousness shall exceed the righteousness of the scribes and Pharisees, ye shall in no case enter into the kingdom of heaven' (Matthew 5:20). That the righteousness that Jesus speaks of here is practical and not imputed is clear from that fact that He spends the rest of the chapter interpreting the Ten Commandments and showing their spiritual and practical breadth (Matthew 5:21–48).

Jesus also understood that His disciples' love had to be governed by obedience and, therefore, law. As such, when He called for His disciples to show their love to Him, He said, 'If ye love me, keep my commandments' (John 14:15). Jesus' reverence for the Ten Commandments shows that, although this command cannot be restricted to them, it certainly includes them.

The rule of life

It is not without Biblical basis, therefore, that Christians have understood the moral law to be a guide to show those who belong to Jesus Christ how to live in obedience to Him.[22] Thomas Boston summed this up when he wrote that

22 The Reformed Church has long referred to this as the third use of the Law. The first use is to restrain wickedness. The second use is that, in showing us how we fall short of its demands, it is 'our schoolmaster to bring us unto Christ, that we might be justified by faith' (Gal. 3:24).

> The law leads to Christ as a Redeemer from its curse and condemnation, and he leads back to the law as a directory, the rule and standard of their obedience to him. ... Believers are still under the law as a rule of life, according to which they are to regulate their hearts and lives. It is the pole star that must direct their course to Heaven, and is of singular use to provoke and excite them to gratitude to Christ, who hath perfectly fulfilled it in their room and stead.[23]

The Christian is, therefore, under law, not in order to gain salvation but as a result of salvation already gained. Obedience to the Ten Commandments is not the way into God's favour. It is, however, the way in which those who have received God's favour show their gratitude.

In his famous book, *Holiness*, J.C. Ryle wrote,

> There is no greater mistake that to suppose that a Christian has nothing to do with the law and the Ten Commandments, because he cannot be justified by keeping them. The same Holy Ghost who convinced the believer of sin by the law, and leads him to Christ for justification, will always lead him to a spiritual use of the law, as a friendly guide, in the pursuit of sanctification.[24]

This is illustrated by the fact that the Ten Commandments were originally given to the Children of Israel after they were redeemed from slavery in Egypt—not before (Exodus 20:1–2). These were laws given to a people already saved, not to a people who had to save themselves through the keeping of them. The moral law, therefore, was a response to Israel's salvation, not the source of it. The same is true for the Christian today—each of the Ten Commandments is to be kept, not in order to gain salvation, but in order to show gratitude for it.

It is notable that the Apostle Paul shows that the believer does not just have an obligation to keep the Law—he also has the ability to keep it. Part of the work of the Spirit is to re-form the image of God in the

---

23 Thomas Boston, *The Complete Works of Thomas Boston*, Vol. 2, p. 69.

24 J. C. Ryle, *Holiness*, Darlington: Evangelical Press, 1979, p. 26.

Christian which was marred in Adam. As such, he tells the Colossians that 'the new man ... is renewed in knowledge after the image of him that created him' (Colossians 3:10). He further defines this new man to the Ephesians as one who 'after God is created in righteousness and true holiness' (Ephesians 4:24). As we have seen, such qualities as knowledge, righteousness and holiness are void if they are not governed by law. That that law is the moral law of Exodus 20 is, hopefully, now self-evident.

The law, then, which Adam failed to keep, and which man has thereafter failed to keep, is now kept—not perfectly, but really—by the man or woman who has been created anew in Christ Jesus. Obedience becomes possible again. The Law was always inscribed upon the heart but, as the writing on an old gravestone becomes far more legible once the stone is restored by a professional, so the Law becomes more legible in both the heart and life of the believer once the image of God is restored in him by the Holy Spirit.

The Sabbath: an obligation

It may seem strange for a chapter on the Christian's duty to observe the Fourth Commandment to dedicate so much space to general law-keeping rather than, specifically, Sabbath-keeping. That, however, is intentional. The believer's clearest warrant for Sabbath observance is not that it is given any specific attention apart from the other Ten Commandments but, rather, that it is included with them. That simple fact—that the observance of the Sabbath is part of the perpetual moral law—is itself enough to make Sabbath keeping a matter of Christian obedience.

> The Christian's duty to keep the Fourth Commandment, then, is not different from his duty to keep any of the other commandments. It may be the most controversial commandment in modern evangelicalism, but it is just as impossible to erase the handwriting of God in this commandment as it is in any of the other nine.[25]

25 Some of the more common modern arguments against Sabbath observance are dealt with in other chapters of this book. However, for a broad discussion of these arguments and engagement with them, see Brian H. Edwards, *The Ten Commandments for Today*, pp. 116–141.

It is certainly true, therefore, to say that Sabbath observance is an obligation for the Christian. Just as Christians are obliged to take up their cross and love their neighbour, and just as they are obliged not to bear false witness nor to steal, so they are obliged to *'Remember the Sabbath Day to keep it holy.'* To keep the Lord's Day free from labour, except in cases of necessity and mercy, is a matter of obedience for the Christian. To dedicate this one day in seven to the public and private worship of God is not a recommendation from God, or a helpful tip—rather, it is a clear commandment.

The Sabbath: a delight

It is important for us to understand, however, that those who have had God's Law graciously re-inscribed upon their hearts do not see Sabbath observance, primarily, as an obligation. When God fills the believer 'with the knowledge of his will in all wisdom and spiritual understanding' (Colossians 1:9), part of the fruit of that wisdom is that we come to see God's Law—and, indeed, all of life—from God's perspective. As a result, we begin to see the purpose of the Law and to understand that 'the law is good, if a man use it lawfully' (1 Timothy 1:8).

If the Law in general is good for man, then, it is no surprise that Jesus could say that 'The Sabbath was made for man, and not man for the Sabbath' (Mark 2:27). God does not need a Sabbath day; He 'neither faints nor is weary' (Isaiah 40:28). Neither does God need the service or worship that we give Him on the Sabbath Day. It is man that needs a Sabbath Day for rest and for worship and it is, therefore, for man that God has purposely designed this good gift.

It is likewise true that all God's laws are a gift. This is why the Psalms are full of the language of loving and delighting in God's Law.[26] In order to understand how the Law can be a source of love and delight, it is important to grasp that it is through Christ-centred law-keeping that man finds true freedom. This is why a Psalmist can say, 'I will walk at liberty: for I seek thy precepts' (Psalm 119:45). Just as the laws of our land today

26 For example, see Psalms 40:8; and 119:16, 24, 35, 47, 97.

allow us to walk the streets or drive our cars with a sense of safety and liberty, so the laws of God's Word allow the believer to be free from the bondage of sin, the tyranny of Satan, and the oppression of self. The only way to be clear from these things is to walk in obedience to both God's gospel invitations and His gospel commands.

All of this is particularly pertinent when it comes to Sabbath observance. This is a commandment which, sadly, many have seen as the very opposite of liberating. It has, at times, been resented, especially by children brought up in Christians homes. For them, it was a day characterised by the fact that they were not allowed to do certain things. In most cases, although not in all, the reason for this was that they did not know the Lord of the Sabbath.

However, when the Christian understands that the obligation of the Sabbath law, like the other laws, is a gift from a loving God that gives spiritual freedom, he will learn, with Isaiah, to 'call the Sabbath a delight' (Isaiah 58:13). When we understand what the Sabbath is and what it is for, we will view it from an entirely new perspective. We will realise that it is a delightful thing 'not to do our own ways, nor find our own pleasure, nor speak our own words' (Isaiah 58:13) for one day a week.

It is liberating for the Christian to have a day dedicated to worship and to rest. It is the Lord's Day, and the world cannot intrude upon it. It is a blessed thing to be able to come away from the things which are lawful and even good on other days, but which so weary our bodies and clog up our minds and hearts. In an article entitled, *The Freedom of Sabbath*, a Christian mother wrote:

> In my home, Sundays mean freedom from school work, yard work, housework, and plain old work. It is freedom from diet, exercise, and running the kids; from errands, to-do lists, and phones.[27]

It is a relief for the workman to down his tools on the Lord's Day and for the office-worker to shut her laptop. It is a delight for the child to

27 Rebecca VanDoodewaard, *The Freedom of Sabbath*, in The Banner of Truth Magazine, December 2020, Edinburgh: The Banner of Truth Trust, 2020, 21.

be under no obligation to do homework for a day. It is a relief for the student to honour God by quitting her studying on a Saturday night and not returning to it until Monday morning, even though she has an exam that day—she can know that God will honour those who honour Him. It is a blessing to switch off televisions and radios, to sign out of from social media, and to take a day off from our normal hobbies and pleasures.

The greatest Sabbath blessing for the Christian, of course, is that the Lord's Day is a day which is set aside for 'the public and private exercises of God's worship'.[28] It is a day dedicated to the most important things in life—to the Word and prayer, church and fellowship, contemplation and meditation. It is a day where other things are set aside, and full attention is given to God.

This is the great force of Isaiah 58:13–14. To 'call the sabbath a delight, the holy of the LORD, honourable' is to 'delight thyself in the LORD'. In fact, it is impossible to properly and Biblically delight ourselves in the Lord without the gift of a Sabbath day which affords us the dedicated and uninterrupted time to do that. This is why Thomas Boston could argue that the Sabbath is the commandment 'on which all religion depends'.[29] It allows us the space in our week to ensure that we are equipped to properly serve God aright, not just on the Sabbath Day but on every day.

Conclusion

In summary, Sabbath observance is undeniably an important element of Christian obedience. As part of the unalterable moral law of God, it is perpetually relevant to both believer and unbeliever alike. The Christian, however, realises that God has made the Sabbath for man and that it is therefore good and liberating. As such, this day becomes a blessing and a delight—not a day to dread or wish away, but a day to anticipate and to cherish.

It is with this sentiment that Thomas Watson could write: 'This commandment was engraven in stone by God's own finger, and it will be

28 Westminster Shorter Catechism, Question 60.

29 Thomas Boston, *The Complete Works of Thomas Boston*, Vol. 2, p. 187.

our comfort to have it engraven in our hearts.'[30] It would be of inestimable benefit for both the Christian individually and the Church corporately if Watson's advice were heeded.

So shall I keep for evermore
  thy law continually.
And, since that I thy precepts seek,
  I'll walk at liberty.
I'll speak thy word to kings, and I
  with shame shall not be moved;
and will delight myself always
  In thy laws, which I loved.

(Psalm 119:44–47)

30 Thomas Watson, *A Body of Divinity*, London: The Banner of Truth Trust, 1959, p. 69.

Chapter 3: A Day to Rest

Rev. Greg MacDonald

Rev. Greg MacDonald is the minister of the Cross congregation of the Free Church of Scotland (Continuing)

The New Testament reminds us that there remains a rest for the people of God (Hebrews 4:9). One of the greatest delights that we should enjoy as Christians is the rest that is provided in Jesus! To be 'in Christ' is to rest in Him, and to know His rest. And the rest that He offers to us will be fully realised in heaven. Meanwhile we have a precious foretaste of this heavenly rest every week, with the reminder of Christ's resurrection, on the Lord's Day.

As a minister, who is seldom as organised and prepared as he intends to be for preaching, I find myself awake quite often after midnight on Saturday evenings. Despite the regret of not being already asleep, there is a real delight in gently slipping into the Lord's Day, knowing that it offers great protection from the things of the world, knowing that I can happily exclude from my thoughts many of the matters that otherwise intrude into my mind. To take up the duties of the day, then, is both a blessing and a pleasure. The restfulness of the day warms our souls and feeds us with expectation for treasures and graces from the hand of our Saviour. It is a sweet thing to wake up in the morning and think, "Oh good, it's Sunday! Today I get to hear the Word of life prepared as a meal for my soul."

But what is this joy, this peace of the Lord's Day, and where has it come from? Let us look further then into the biblical origin of the Lord's Day and take our guidance from Scripture.

1. It is a day cleared of our usual labour

Very much of the rest of the Lord's Day is that on this day we are liberated from the usual burden of work. Adam was mandated to work in the garden of Eden. Even in paradise, man was made to be occupied and not idle. He was given the seventh day as a Sabbath (rest), following the pattern of the Creator, who took six days to create the world, and ceased from His labour on the seventh day.

This blessed pattern for mankind was a gift of God; it was typical of the generous and kind nature of the Lord God. And the foresight of a weekly rest was soon evident when Adam sinned, and now his labours were not the gentle relaxed ventures of tending a garden without thorns or weeds. Now he must work in the sweat of his brow. Now the very soil that he tilled seemed to work against his every endeavour.

To be given then a weekly rest was not only a Creation appointment, but also a wonderfully kind provision from an all-knowing Maker. The Creation Sabbath was undoubtedly a sweet release for mankind from the toil of his usual workload. None of that means the Sabbath then was to be treated as an optional extra, a generous opt-in blessing should you feel the need for it. Quite the reverse.

In giving the summary of the moral law in Exodus 20, the Fourth Commandment is one of the longest of the ten. Ample column inches are given over to what it means to 'Remember the sabbath day to keep it holy.' In simple terms, the Fourth Commandment requires us to cease from our ordinary business, our usual occupations, and instead set the time apart as holy time, time to be devoted to the Lord and His worship.

There are those who suggest that this law was relevant only to the Hebrews. Certainly, it was given to the Israelites as they made their exodus from Egypt. That is not in doubt. But that this rule obliged all of mankind is clear from the reason annexed to it in verse 11: 'For in six days the LORD made heaven and earth, the sea, and all that in them is, and rested the seventh day: wherefore the LORD blessed the sabbath day, and hallowed it.' God rooted the demand for obedience to this command, not on something unique to the Hebrews, but on an obligation drawn from the creation of the human race.

The order then is plain: we clear away our activities, such as our housework, our leisure, our employment, or our schooling, to truly rest from these things. Only when we lay down the ordinary occupations of our hands, are we free to embrace the delight of the rest given to us by our God.

If we investigate a little further in the Old Testament for the practical applications of this rule to the lives of the people of God, we do not have to employ any arbitrary interpretation of the text to discover the way the Jews understood this.

Consider the man who went out to gather sticks on the Sabbath Day, mentioned in Numbers 15:32ff. The Israelites knew this was wrong, and detained the man, bringing him before Moses and Aaron. However, they were not clear as to the severity of the offence. They were not sure what punishment should follow. No case law had been given directly about this. Was it to be taken with grave seriousness, or not? The Lord directly answered the point, speaking to Moses, and requiring the man to be stoned to death by the congregation. That certainly made clear the seriousness with which God took this matter.

Another case is perhaps better known. At the rebuilding of the walls of Jerusalem, in the post-exile period, Nehemiah had to deal with a Sabbath-breaking problem (Nehemiah 13:15). The matters at issue were treading the wine presses, bringing in the sheaves, loading up the animals, bringing all the wares into Jerusalem, and then proceeding to sell them on the Sabbath. It is instructive to note that it is not only the Jews who were guilty. Verse 16 notes also men of Tyre, a Gentile city, who were also guilty of profiting on the Sabbath day.

This activity destroyed the rest gifted by God, and intended for all mankind, Jew and Gentile. And the yet the guilt is especially noted regarding the Lord's people. In verse 18 Nehemiah rehearses the history of Sabbath breaking that had cost them their land and exile in the first place.

Now in these two examples neither gathering sticks (presumably for firewood) or selling wares in Jerusalem were morally wrong actions. On any other day they were perfectly permissible and acceptable. We notice then that the Old Testament saw a very clear application of the Sabbath principle in setting aside legitimate ordinary work in order to most enjoy and benefit from the holy rest of the seventh day.

We also notice from these examples the idea of the corporate Sabbath. Even where the keeping of one day in seven holy to the Lord is maintained today, how common to find that it is thought to be a purely personal, individual choice! Such an individualised rest was utterly foreign to the people of the Old Testament.

Let's go back to the commandment itself once more, in Exodus 20. Notice how much of the command is about the corporate communal enjoyment of this rest. It extends far beyond the individual. Everyone in their sphere of influence is included: family, servants, workers, animals, and even short-term guests, whom you might barely know. If they are under your roof, and under your influence, then it is expected that the Sabbath rest is offered and extended to them every bit as much as to the individual.

Now look how far this extended. It extended in the first instance to the whole community concerning themselves with the activity of another householder. If we hold only to an individualistic view of the Sabbath, then the man gathering sticks is not interfering with the Sabbath-keeping of any other Israelite. They are free to do as they please. Nonetheless the people act corporately in seeking to address this breach of the communal rest gifted to them by their Creator and covenant God.

In the second example, we find that Nehemiah, acting as ruler, enforces the Sabbath command upon the nation, and even extends it to the non-Jewish traders from Tyre. He clearly interpreted the Sabbath command, about the stranger 'within thy gates' to include a responsibility towards those of other nations and beliefs, who were under his influence as the civil magistrate.

Indeed, it is not only men who took this communal view of Sabbath-keeping in the Old Testament. The Lord Himself surely was the origin of this broader community-wide rest. We see this when the Lord punishes, not individual Sabbath-breakers, but all of Judah, for their breaking of His Fourth Commandment, when the people were carried away to Babylon: 'To fulfil the word of the LORD by the mouth of Jeremiah, until the land had enjoyed her sabbaths: for as long as she lay desolate she kept sabbath, to fulfil threescore and ten years' (2 Chronicles 36:21; Jeremiah 25:12; 29:10).

It is clear that, at least in Old Testament times, the Sabbath Day was given to be a rest for mankind, in order the better to keep a holy day of worship to the Lord.

Other contributors to this book will deal much more extensively with the positive activities of the Sabbath, particularly the redemptive emphasis that follows from the second issuing of the commandments in Deuteronomy (compare Deuteronomy 5:12ff. with Exodus 20:8ff.).

We now come to the question of whether this Old Testament ideal of a blessed resting from secular labours to enjoy a day of worship is carried over into the New Testament, and indeed into the present.

2. It is a day commended and claimed by Christ

We come now to consider the words of the Saviour in the Gospels. We will give special attention to the opening thirteen verses of Matthew 12.

I remember several years ago sitting in the local Town Hall in Stornoway. Every summer the local LDOS branch would organise a public rally. The hall would regularly be filled with hundreds of supporters. The speaker, Rev. George MacAskill, in addressing us used an illustration I have never forgotten. He spoke of a man taking a worn-out, old washing machine to the dump. Its bearings were gone, and it was old and rusty. But on the way to the dump, the man noticed that the wiring was frayed and dangerous. Would he stop to fix it?

Of course not—why would he, if he is about to dump it! Then we were directed to the number of times the Lord 'fixes' the Pharisees' understanding of the Lord's Day. How often in the Gospels the Lord carefully realigned the mistaken and legalistic views of the Sabbath promoted by the Pharisees. Now if He (as Lord of the Sabbath) was about to dump it, then why bother? It is precisely because the Lord Jesus knew that the Sabbath principle would continue and persist that He took the time to restore true Sabbath-keeping ideals. For the same reason the Holy Spirit chose to preserve these teachings in the inspired record.

The setting is almost a rural idyll. Jesus was walking and talking. His disciples were listening and learning and following the Master. We imagine the warm Mediterranean sun, the soft breeze, and the wholesome atmosphere. What a sweet time of fellowship it must have been! The disciples of the Lord, being hungry, plucked some ears of corn, and ate as they went. This drew the ire of the eagle-eyed Pharisees, who protested that the disciples had broken the law. Notice the correction that Jesus issued.

First, He justified what His disciples did. Their actions were not interfering with the Sabbath principle. They were resting from their usual labours. They were not fishing or tax collecting or wood-working. Their being hungry was no sin, and satisfying that hunger was no sin.

Jesus appealed to two separate Old Testament examples. Note what He was doing. He was not dispensing with the Sabbath principle. He was correcting the legalism of the Pharisees. Jesus did not now claim that the Sabbath rest is over, and that they should be harvesting the corn. He instead affirmed that to condemn the plucking off the heads of corn as you walk past was a ludicrous and an unwarranted condemnation of His disciples.

Notice the development of the chapter. In the first incident the Lord defended His disciples; in the second He exemplified true Sabbath-keeping and provided a pattern for His people to follow. In this second incident, the scene had moved to the local synagogue. The sick man was pushed into prominence. The heartless legalists were ready to imply that healing on the Sabbath is wrong. Jesus was utterly unmoved by their pressure. He first shone a light on their hypocrisy and then proceeded to heal the poor man.

What we notice then is that Jesus was pulling the Jews back from a very harsh, unkind, ritualistic view of the day of rest. This was not what it was ever meant to be. It is a day to enjoy. It is a day to do good. For the Pharisee the Sabbath was so stuffed with rules and regulations that it had lost its restfulness. It was a day of oppressive scrutiny, accusations, and mean-spiritedness. How far from the Old Testament view of a day in which to delight, a day of rest, a day where we enjoy the gift of more time for the adoration of our Saviour God!

Yet we must notice what Jesus did not do. He did not pull down the Sabbath. He did not deny it. He did not obliterate the distinction of a special day of rest. Yes, He claims Lordship over the Sabbath (v. 8), but

He was not claiming authority over it to decimate it. Instead, the Saviour removed the unwarranted intrusions and arbitrary restrictions imposed by the Pharisees. This was not and never had been the rest that His Father had gifted to His people.

In the second incident, the Lord chose to heal a man with a withered hand. He had entered their synagogue, and it was still the Sabbath day. In this event, we see the other side of the coin. In the first case Jesus lifted unwarranted restrictions; in the second case, He modelled the sort of behaviour that is called for during the rest of the Sabbath.

We have so far addressed the rest from what it is negatively. What is to be set aside, what is to be kept out of the resting of the Sabbath. What then is required? The Sabbath rest was never intended to be idleness. Doing nothing is not the same as a holy resting.

The Saviour's pattern in Matthew 12:9–13 helps us to uncover how the Lord kept the Sabbath. Notice then that the setting is not incidental. Sometimes it is all too easy to miss the context and rush on to the miracle—in this case the healing of the withered hand. But notice that the Saviour went to worship. This was how He chose to spend the day: in the worship of His God. This was how He chose to spend every Sabbath Day. There are no records in Scripture of Him neglecting public worship, either at the synagogue on the weekly Sabbath, or at the temple during the special feasts of worship. We can then safely conclude that the rest of the Sabbath is primarily set aside as a resting from labour, to enable a clear period for the worship of God.

Notice that this was not the same as private worship. The Sabbath is particularly set aside for the public corporate worship of the Lord. Every day, the believer will bow and privately worship his Redeemer. If they live with others in the home, then family worship should be a daily blessing. The Saviour never neglected private worship. He often went away from the crowds to worship and pray through the night. But when the weekly Sabbath came round, He repeatedly associated Himself with the gatherings for public worship which that weekly Sabbath day required.

In doing this the Lord Jesus modelled for us the best pattern for the day. But the incident before us soon develops in another direction. Whether by design of the Pharisees or not, they seem to have been expecting both this injured man and the Saviour to be present. They are watching for His reaction. Despite the pressure, the Saviour does not hesitate for a moment. He is perfectly ready to do good to this man. He is perfectly content to include works of mercy in His Sabbath rest and alongside even His Sabbath worship. The Saviour finds no contradiction or proscription against such care and kindness.

It is important to notice that Jesus does not here extend or adjust the rules for the Sabbath. He merely demonstrates the liberties of the day, in a way that had been lost through the legalism of the Pharisees. He does not amend the Sabbath regulations. He correctly states and applies them. He moves seamlessly from worship to helping a poor sick man: 'It is lawful to do well on the sabbath days' (v. 12).

The two incidents give us a full picture of what this rest involves. Our Westminster Shorter Catechism covers these twin aspects when it makes clear the exemption of works of necessity and mercy from the sort of rest that is required on the Lord's Day.

At no point does the Lord set aside the Old Testament regulations. Instead, He asserts boldly that He is Lord of the Sabbath. He sets the pattern, and He issues the requirements of the Sabbath. Yet as Lord of the day, He does not even begin to suggest it is to be set aside. He clarifies it from the confusion of His enemies. He exemplifies it in His twin actions of going to the synagogue to worship and healing the sick whilst He was there. In claiming Lordship over the Day, the Lord commends to us His own actions as the standard, modelling for us how we are to keep the rest that is inherent to the Sabbath.

There are those who believe that the Sabbath regulations ended with the Cross. They choose to set aside the example and claim of the Lord, noting that this behaviour takes place prior to the Cross, and therefore under Old Testament regulations. If that alone was sufficient basis to set aside the teaching and example of Christ, then what relevance would any of His acts in the Gospel records have for us?

Nonetheless it brings us to our closing section for this chapter.

3. It is a day continued after the cross

It has been clearly set out elsewhere in this book that there is a transition from the seventh day to the first, and that the Lord's Day now amply covers the terms of the Fourth Commandment. It is my purpose here to draw attention to the continuation of the rest itself in New Testament times and into the age between the two Comings of Christ.

We might first notice that the rest called for by the Sabbath laws, and exemplified and clarified by the Saviour, is no less relevant or worthwhile today than it was after the fall of man, or after the giving of the Law at Sinai, or indeed after the birth of Christ in first century Palestine.

The rest called for was a rest that set aside ordinary secular employment and duties. It was a rest that was devoted to corporate worship. And it was a rest that encouraged works of mercy and compassion. The laws of the Old Testament famously fall into three categories. There were *judicial* laws given to Israel as a nation, which expired with the passing of the nation in AD 70. General principles from these laws can be applied today. There were *ceremonial* laws—such as the priestly laws, the laws about the offerings, and the tabernacle/temple. These laws were typical, given as visual signs of the work of Christ and His Church. They are fulfilled in Christ, and so their obligation has ceased. There are *moral* laws, laws based not on the welfare of the nation of Israel, nor on the patterning of the Cross to come, but on the moral character of God Himself. Such laws have not passed away, and cannot pass away, because God remains constant.

The Fourth Commandment belongs with the moral law. It is part of the summary of the moral law found in the Ten Commandments. It is found in the summaries of the moral law in both Exodus 20 and Deuteronomy 5. Mankind still needs to clear away jobs and duties, and worship God. Without an appointed day of rest, that becomes impossible. The Sabbath principle of a weekly rest cannot pass away unless the obligation to worship God together has also ceased.

Notice, secondly, that the Sabbath principle is nowhere rescinded throughout the New Testament. Arguments from silence are seldom convincing by themselves, but this silence is certainly one of the more powerful ones of Scripture. There are those who undervalue the Old Testament, by considering that only when an Old Testament principle is re-stated in the New Testament is it to be considered binding. This is a serious mistake. The Word of God is one. We must not set aside any of its commandments without explicit warrant so to do. Yet nothing in the New Testament suggests that the Church set aside corporate public worship in favour of individual private worship. Nothing in the Acts or the Epistles teaches us that the need for rest is done away with. The rest of the Sabbath Day was a rich blessing in the Old Testament. It is only when we have a Pharisaic attitude towards the Sabbath and hold it to be a burden to be endured, instead of a delight to be enjoyed, that we wish to set it aside. The insistence on a continued Sabbath rest for the people of God is in no way a Pharisaic position. It is the opposite.

Thirdly notice that the Sabbath principle is assumed to continue after the cross and resurrection. In Matthew 24:20 the Lord himself references the Sabbath, when He offers guidance with regard to prayer:

> "But pray ye that your flight be not in the winter, neither on the Sabbath day:"

Now whatever interpretation is taken of the chapter as a whole, all are agreed that it references a period chronologically later than the death of Christ, but earlier than his return. As such we find that the Saviour makes a clear reference to the Sabbath day continuing after His death and resurrection. Were the Sabbath simply abolished by his death, as a merely ceremonial part of the Law, then His counsel would be redundant. Clearly no Christian could contemplate such a position!

Finally, and most pertinently of all, notice that the principle of rest, far from being rescinded, is in fact restated and reclaimed in the New Testament. For this we turn back to Hebrews 4. It is impossible to read the opening eleven verses without being struck by the frequency of the mention of rest. What comes out in some translations (but not all) is that the 'rest' mentioned in verse 9 is a totally different word from the rest mentioned throughout the rest of the section. It is explicitly a Sabbath rest

(Greek = *sabbatismos*). The epistle makes clear that the rest is a promise (v. 1). The rest offered in the Old Testament to the children of Israel was a promise. It was patterned by the entering into the Promised Land, led by Joshua (KJV here uses Jesus, as the Greek form of Joshua's Hebrew name).

But was that it? Was that all the rest that God's people needed? Of course not, as verse 8 makes clear. The Promised Land was a picture of true spiritual rest. What we find in Hebrews is that we enter God's rest by faith (v. 3). That is to say that we have rest for our souls in Jesus and in His salvation. By faith we receive the benefits of His redemption. We rest in Christ.

But what is also clear is that there is more rest to be had! There is a fuller resting in Christ that awaits us in heaven. As surely as God entered into the seventh day rest of Creation, and so made that day of rest for mankind, so too the Lord Jesus has entered into His rest by completing His great work of redemption. He has now ceased from His own works and entered His rest.

And it is the sure hope of the believer to join with Him and to enter and enjoy that higher, heavenly rest with the Saviour one day. Again, a later chapter of this book will explore in greater depth this blessed promise! So let us get back to verse 9: 'There remaineth therefore a (Sabbath) rest to the people of God.'

If we read through the experiences of past Christian writers, or if we speak to present Christian companions, or even if we reflect upon our own Christian experiences, we won't take long to find the sentiment that a Lord's Day was just heavenly!

It is evident that Joshua taking Israel into Canaan was not the full promised rest to the believer. It is equally evident that even present faith in Christ is not the full rest promised and held out to the Christian. It is not yet heaven. And the Lord's Day, maintaining the principle of the Old Testament Sabbath, is then this foretaste of heaven on earth. It is a promise of the more that is to come!

Chapter 4: A Day to Believe

Rev. Malcolm Macleod

Rev. Malcolm Macleod is the minister of the Shawbost congregation of the Free Church of Scotland

Introduction

The Fourth Commandment has a pivotal place in the Decalogue or the Ten Commandments. The observance of the Fourth Commandment, and the principle of the one-day-of-rest-in-seven observed on the seventh day of the week as the weekly Sabbath, had a pivotal place in the life of the people of God in the Old Testament. The observance of the Fourth Commandment, and the principle of the one-day-of-rest-in-seven, has a pivotal place in the life of the New Testament Church, with the observance of the Sabbath rest on the first day of the week, the Lord's Day.

We are faced with the challenge that the observance of the Fourth Commandment, and the principle of the one-day-of-rest-in-seven, no longer applies because the Lord Jesus has fulfilled the Law and because He has established the rest to which the Sabbath rest pointed. How do we address this challenge? How does the Fourth Commandment, with the requirement for a one-day-of-rest in seven, apply to the Church today? What is the relevance of a Commandment given by the Lord to the children of Israel in c. 1446 BC to our twenty-first century church and world?

In this chapter we will look at the abiding validity of the Fourth Commandment and at the Sabbath as a day to believe. We will do so by examining some the teaching of the Old Testament and of the New Testament, showing the continuity in the observance of the Commandment and focusing on the development of its observance after the resurrection of the Lord Jesus from the dead.

Biblical revelation

The lens with which we read and understand the Bible—our biblical hermeneutic—is critical to the discovery of the truths and values of the Word of God. There are three related concepts which can help us place the subject of the Fourth Commandment, and the one-day-of-rest-in-seven principle, into the context of progressive, redemptive revelation and that of biblical theology.

The first key term is *protology*. Protology is the study of the origin of first things and refers to God's purpose for humankind. The purpose of God for man is set out in Genesis 1–2. God created the heavens and the earth as the perfect environment for man. God created man in His own image and likeness. God saw that 'It is not good that man should be alone' (Genesis 2:18). He made a 'helper comparable to him' to be his bride with whom he was to fulfil his creation purpose. He placed Adam and Eve in the paradise of the Garden of Eden. Adam was to keep the Garden; he was to spread the paradise environment to cover the whole creation; and he was to fill the earth with the humankind in the likeness and image of God.

The second key term is *eschatology*. Eschatology is the doctrine of the last things. It deals with the teaching that God's sovereignty, and control of history, means that the world as we know it is moving towards a definite final goal. This final goal lies beyond this world when a new order of affairs will be established, which will not be subject to any further change but will instead have the permanent character of the eternal.

The concept of eschatology is closely related to protology. Protology, and God's purpose for man, predicts eschatology. It will help us to have a better understanding of the principle of the Sabbath rest if we recognise that there was eschatology before there was sin. There was a terminus, an eschatological goal, to the Adam's labours before the fall recorded in Genesis 3. At the conclusion of the creation week, after six days of labour, God rested from his labours on the seventh day. He blessed the seventh day and sanctified it. It was now the duty of the Adam to follow his heavenly Father's example. Adam lived out his life in the same seven-day cycle as that of his Creator; he was to perform his own labours in obedience to the covenant of works.

The third key term is *soteriology*. Soteriology is the doctrine of salvation. God made a *covenant of works* with the 'first man Adam' (1 Corinthians 15:45) 'wherein life was promised to him, and in him to his posterity, upon condition of perfect and personal obedience' (Westminster Confession of Faith, Chapter 7.2). This First Adam failed his probationary period in the Garden of Eden, he fell into sin. He failed to finish the work given to him in the terms of the covenant of works. He was, therefore, driven out of the Garden under the curse of the broken covenant. The prospect of following his Creator into the divinely appointed eschatological rest accordingly was lost to him.

Soteriology is about the mission of God in coming to rescue fallen humankind and thereby putting back on track His eternal purpose and goal for His people. The story of redemption commences in Genesis 3:15. The Lord was pleased to make a second covenant, 'commonly called the Covenant of Grace' (Westminster Confession of Faith, 7.3), with the *'Last Adam'* (1 Corinthians 15:45), the Lord Jesus Christ. This second covenant speaks of God's intervention to rescue humankind from the consequences of the fall through the redemptive work of Christ, and the application of His redemptive work to the elect people of God by the Holy Spirit. The Last Adam succeeds where the First Adam failed. He is obedient even to death on a cross (Philippians 2:8–9). He will fulfil the creation mandate with the help of His bride, the Church, through the propagation of the gospel.

The relationship

The relationship between protology, eschatology and soteriology, and the order in which the Word of God speaks of them, underlies our understanding of the permanent validity of the Fourth Commandment. 'It is not biblical to hold that eschatology is a sort of appendix to soteriology, a consummation of the saving work of God. Eschatology is not necessarily bound up with soteriology. So conceived, it does not take into account that a whole chapter of eschatology is written before sin. Thus, it is not merely an omission to ignore pre-redemptive eschatology; it is to place the sequel in the wrong place.'[31] Soteriology is not the end. The realisation of God's purposes of redemption 'is the means to the end of realising His purpose of creation'.[32] Eschatology is the terminus to which the purpose of God moves forward under His direction and now, with the fall of the First Adam, by way of the finished work of the Last Adam, the Lord Jesus Christ.

The Sabbatical principle

The Fourth Commandment principle of one-day-of-rest-in-seven is embedded in the doctrine of creation. This is clear from the words of God to Moses at Sinai: 'For in six days the LORD made the heavens and the earth, the sea, and all that is in them, and rested the seventh day. Therefore, the LORD blessed the Sabbath day and hallowed it' (Exodus 20:11).

The Divine rest

God created the perfect environment for humankind in six days. The 'heavens and the earth, and all the host of them, were finished' (Genesis 2:1). In words that are a precursor to the cry of the Lord Jesus on the cross (John 19:30), we read that 'God ended [finished] His work which He had done' (Genesis 2:2). God then 'rested on the seventh day from all His work which He had done' (Genesis 2:2). By resting, God declared his creative activity to be finished. Here is eschatology.

The divine rest was a rest of achievement. It was a case of mission accomplished. The divine rest was not a time of inactivity. It was a time during which God took delight in a creation working according to divine design. A succession of judgements expressing the builder's pleasure in the work of each day led to the final verdict of delighted satisfaction: 'God saw everything that he had made, and indeed it was very good' (Genesis 1:31). God is portrayed as 'the cosmic builder who attained to the royal rest of the Sabbath Day'.[33]

---

31 Vos, G. (2001), *The Eschatology of the Old Testament*, p. 73

32 J. V. Fesko (2007), *Last Things First*, pp. 190–191.

33 Meredith G. Kline (2006), *Kingdom Prologue—Genesis Foundations for a Covenantal Worldview*, p. 38.

The first Adam

The doctrine of one day of rest in seven is central to man's relationship with God. Man is the divine image-bearer (Genesis 1:27). The first Adam is tasked to multiply and fill the earth with his offspring bearing the image of God, and to spread the conditions of the Edenic paradise to cover the whole of God's creation (Genesis 1:26–28). There was a mission to be accomplished. The mission was to be accomplished as the first Adam followed his heavenly Father's example—he lived out his life in the same seven-day cycle as that of his Creator; he was to perform his own labours in obedience to the covenant of works in six days and then rest on the seventh day.

A creation ordinance

The Fourth Commandment principle of one day of rest in seven is embedded in Adam's relationship with God in the first creation. This is implied, if not clearly stated, in the Westminster Confession of Faith—'As it is the law of nature, that, in general, a due proportion of time be set apart for the worship of God…' (21.7). 'The meaning of the original Sabbath (Genesis 2:2) is mirrored in the Sabbath ordinance (Genesis 2:3), the record of which emphasises that the Sabbath is set apart as sacred to the Creator. It belongs to the Lord of the covenant and it witnesses to God's ultimate proprietorship of the land and his lordship over the total life of man. Observance of the Sabbath by man is thus a confession that Yahweh is his Lord and Lord of all lords. Sabbath-keeping expresses man's commitment to the service of his Lord.' [34] The message of the Fourth Commandment refers man back to his most essential relationship, that is, his relationship with God.

A covenant sign

The Sabbath as a creation ordinance becomes a soteriological sign in the unfolding of God's relationship with his people. The Sabbath Day commandment is given to Israel at Mount Sinai. The identity of the

---

34 Meredith G. Kline (2006), *Kingdom Prologue*, p.39.

Lawgiver, the context of the Commandment, and who the recipients are, is set out in the prologue to the Ten Commandments in Exodus 20:1–2. The Lawgiver at Mount Sinai is the covenant God of Israel—'I am the LORD your God…' (Exodus 20:2). The Lawgiver places his Law in the environment of grace—'who brought you out of the land of Egypt, out of the house of bondage' (Exodus 20:2). The recipients/hearers are the covenant people of God—'This is the blood of the covenant which the LORD has made with you according to all these words' (Exodus 24:8). The Fourth Commandment has a soteriological element and an eschatological element to it—it looks forward to the redemption proclaimed in the sacrificial system of the tabernacle. It also looks forward to the rest of the Promised Land.

As a soteriological sign, the Sabbath also now functions as a sign of the covenant between God and His people. This was clearly stated by the Lord to Moses at Mount Sinai—'It is a sign between Me and the children of Israel forever…' (Exodus 31:17). The observance of the Sabbath Day rest is also permanently binding for them—'the children of Israel shall keep the Sabbath, to observe the Sabbath throughout their generations as a perpetual covenant' (Exodus 31:16). The Lord who redeems is the Lord who has originally created, and who is determined to renew his fallen creation and guide it to the goal of his pleasing. Far from there being a disjunction between creation and salvation, they are intimately linked together, and that is especially true in the Sabbath-sign that the Lord instituted for his people.[35] The Sabbath is a permanent marker and identifier of the covenant people of God.

The moral law

The Fourth Commandment is an essential element of the moral law as it is summarised in the Ten Commandments. The moral law states what God commands and desires to see prevailing in the world he has brought into existence. The moral law is a reflection of God Himself and arises from His character. The requirements of the moral law express the unchanging

35 J. L. Mackay (2001), *Exodus*, p. 520.

will of God as Creator. The moral law 'is the declaration of the will of God to mankind, directing and binding everyone to personal, perfect, and perpetual conformity and obedience thereunto' (Larger Catechism 93; see also the Westminster Confession of Faith, 19.5).

The Fourth Commandment, and the necessity for a Sabbath rest, cannot therefore be revoked. This is clearly and unequivocally stated in the Westminster Confession of Faith: 'As it is the law of nature, that, in general, a due proportion of time be set apart for the worship of God; so, in His Word, by a positive, moral, and perpetual commandment, binding all men, in all ages, He hath particularly appointed one day in seven, for a Sabbath, to be kept holy unto Him...' (21:7).

This is emphatically stated by J.D. Currid in his commentary on the book of Exodus: 'the moral law doth forever bind all, as well justified persons as others, to the obedience thereof; and that, not only in regard of the matter contained in it, but also in respect of the authority of God the Creator, who gave it. Neither doth Christ, in the gospel, any way dissolve, but much strengthen this obligation.'[36]

The New Testament

The New Testament Church is defined by the fulfilment of the Old Testament Messianic promises, by the new covenant established by the Lord Jesus Christ, and by the pouring out of the Holy Spirit on the Day of Pentecost. The fulfilment of the promises, and the new covenant epoch of the Church, does not invalidate or abrogate the Fourth Commandment and the requirement to take one day of Sabbath rest in the week. However, what we do find in the life of the New Testament Church is a new order and a new practice.

The new order

The new order is established after the resurrection of the Lord Jesus Christ from the dead. The one day of Sabbath rest in the week is observed on the first day of the week. This new practice is clearly stated in the Westminster

36 J. D. Currid (2001), *A Study Commentary of Exodus*, Vol. 2, p. 34.

Confession of Faith: 'He hath particularly appointed one day in seven, for a Sabbath, to be kept holy unto Him, which, from the beginning of the world to the resurrection of Christ, was the last day of the week; and, from the resurrection of Christ, was changed into the first day of the week, which, in Scripture, is called the Lord's Day, and is to be continued to the end of the world, as the Christian Sabbath' (21:7).

The authority

When we examine the biblical data regarding this revised practice, we do not find a positive New Testament law re-enacting the directions for the Sabbath Day of rest. However, our biblical warrant for the observance of the first day of the week as the Lord's Day in obedience to the Fourth Commandment is based on two principles. First, the example and precedent set by the Lord Jesus Christ and his apostles is as binding as their command. In other words, example may be as valid and instructive a guide to duty as precept. Secondly, there is the principle of good and necessary inference. This principle is clearly stated in the Westminster Confession of Faith: 'The whole counsel of God, concerning all things necessary for His own glory, man's salvation, faith, and life, is either expressly set down in Scripture, or by good and necessary consequence may be deduced from Scripture' (1:6).

We observe the first day of the week as the weekly day of rest in obedience to the Fourth Commandment on the basis that the Lord Jesus and his apostles did, from the day of the resurrection of Christ, hallow this first day as the Lord's Day and the weekly Sabbath.

The biblical data

The disciples underwent what seems to be a natural transition from observing the seventh day of the week as the weekly Sabbath to the practice of observing the first day of the week as the day set apart for the Lord. They commenced the observance of the first day of the week as the Lord's Day on the very day of Christ's resurrection. The disciples were assembled on 'the same day at evening, being the first day of the week' (John 20:19) when the Lord Jesus appeared to them. The Lord Jesus appeared to them again—'after eight days his disciples were again inside ... Jesus came and stood in the midst' (John 20:26). By the Jews' method of counting the time, which always included in their count the days on which the period began and ended, the 'eighth day', or full week from the disciples' first meeting, brings us again to the first day of the week. This new practice bears the stamp of approval of the Lord Jesus himself. We see this from his regular appearances to them on that day, and also in the blessing he bestowed upon them when he 'breathed on them, and said to them, "Receive the Holy Spirit"' (John 20:22).

We see this practice continuing in the life of the Church in the New Testament (cf. Acts 1:13–14; 1 Corinthians 16:2; Acts 20:7; Revelation 1:10. The evidence is compelling. From the example and precedent set by the Lord Jesus Christ and his apostles, and from the good and necessary inference arising from the above examples, we can conclude that the practice of the New Testament Church with regard to the Fourth Commandment was to observe the first day of the week as the Lord's Day, the Christian Sabbath.

A new creation

The resurrection is the key turning point in redemptive history. The Lord Jesus 'finished' (John 19:30) the work that Father had given him. On the first day of the week (Mark 16:2), God the Father raised his Son from the dead by the power of the Holy Spirit (Romans 8:11). He ascended and was exalted at the right hand of God, ushering in the last stage of redemptive history, and inaugurating the new creation.

'The resurrection of Christ is the beginning of the new and final world-order, an order described as spiritual and heavenly. It is the dawn of the new creation, and the start of the eschatological age.'[37] 'Christ's death and resurrection mark the turning of the ages, so much so that nothing, absolutely nothing, is any longer the same, the old has gone, the new has come.'[38] In the words of N. T. Wright, 'Jesus' public career is to be

37 Richard B. Gaffin, Jnr (1987), *Resurrection and Redemption*, pp. 89–90.
38 Gordon D. Fee (1999), *God's Empowering Presence*, p. 330.

understood as the completion of the original creation, with the resurrection as the start of the new.'[39]

The Sabbath principle is therefore applied to the day of Christ's resurrection, the first day of the redeemed new creation and the first step towards never-ending rest, joy, and satisfaction of eternity. 'As the author of the new creation, Jesus ministers the benefits of his saving work through the Word and the sacraments. This is seen in the repeated revelation of Jesus on the first day of the week, both before his ascension (Matthew 28:1–8; Mark 16:1–8; Luke 24:1–49; John 20:1–29) and afterwards (Acts 2; Revelation 1:10). This is why the early church continued to meet on the first day (Acts 20:7; 1 Corinthians 16:2).'[40]

A new man

The finished work of the first creation was a perfect environment for man created in the image of God. The finished work of the new creation provides the perfect environment and conditions for the re-creation of man in the image of God and the purpose of God to be realised.

The critical change is clearly stated by Paul—'For as in Adam all die, even so in Christ all shall be made alive' (1 Corinthians 15:22); 'even when we were dead in trespasses, made us alive together with Christ (by grace you have been saved)' (Ephesians 2:5). This is nothing less than a new creation—'if anyone is in Christ, he is a new creation; old things have passed away; behold, all things have become new' (2 Corinthians 5:17). The children of God are the divine image bearers—'you have put off the old man with his deeds, and have put on the new man who is renewed in knowledge according to the image of Him who created him' (Colossians 3:9–10).

A new covenant

The unrepeatable event of Pentecost recorded in Acts 2 is foundational to the New Testament Church. It is the fulfilment of the Old Testament prophecies concerning the outpouring of the Spirit (Joel 2:28). The new covenant is the age of the Holy Spirit as proclaimed repeatedly by the

39 N. T. Wright (2003), *The Resurrection of the Son of God*, p. 440.
40 Andrew Clarke (2007), *Love Rules—The Ten Commandments for the 21st Century*, p. 46.

Old Testament prophets (Ezekiel 36:25–27; Jeremiah 31:31–34). That the apostles saw the Day of Pentecost as the day of the new covenant is evident from the words of Peter when he proclaimed, 'this is what was spoken by the prophet Joel' (Acts 2:16), to explain the unique events. This is also clear in Peter's proclamation of the gospel and the place of the Spirit in personal salvation (Acts 2:38).

A close examination of the celebration the Day of Pentecost shows that God chose to mark the inauguration of the new covenant on the first day of the week, the Lord's Day. The Day of Pentecost was appointed by the Lord under the old covenant (cf. Leviticus 23:15–16; Deuteronomy 16:9–10). According to the Word of God, the appointment of the Day of Pentecost was counted from the day after the Sabbath, the first day of the week. From this first day of the week, they were to count seven weeks complete, and the fiftieth day was to be the Day of Pentecost. Bearing in mind the Jews method of counting time, we see that the fiftieth day brings us to the first day of the week, corresponding to our Lord's Day. The God of heaven marked the first day of the week as the Lord's Day with the birth of the New Testament Church in fulfilment of the new covenant promise.

The event of Pentecost, says American theologian R.L. Dabney, 'was meant by God as a forcible precedent, establishing the Lord's day as our Christian Sabbath'.[41] We must learn, Dabney goes on to say, 'that the day selected by God for setting up the gospel dispensation and for the great Pentecostal outpouring was the Lord's day—a significant and splendid testimony to the sacred honour it was intended to have in the Christian ages. This epoch was indeed the creation of a new world in the spiritual sense. The work was equal in glory and everlasting moment to that first creation which caused "the morning stars to sing together and all the sons of God to shout for joy". Well might God substitute the first day for the seventh when the first day had now become the sign of two separate events, the rising of Christ and the founding of the new dispensation, either of which is as momentous and blessed to us as the world's foundation.'[42]

41 R. L. Dabney (1982), *Discussions*, Vol. 1, p. 532.
42 R. L. Dabney (1982), *Discussions*, Vol. 1, pp. 531–532.

The new heavens and new earth

How do we answer the objection that because we find our rest by faith in Jesus Christ (Matthew 11:28–29) the observance of the Fourth Commandment no longer applies? This question takes us back to the concept of *eschatology* (the doctrine of the last things), and the relationship between *protology* (God's purpose for mankind), *eschatology* and *soteriology* (the mission of God to save mankind from the consequences of the fall). Referring back to the words of J. V. Fesko, 'soteriology is not the end. The realisation of God's purposes of redemption is the means to the end of realising His purpose of creation.' [43]

Where the Word of God places us now in the timeline of His plan and purpose is critical to our understanding of the Lord's Day and in preparing an answer to the objection above. We look back upon the accomplished work of Christ. 'We, therefore, first celebrate the rest in principle procured by Christ, although the Sabbath also still remains a sign looking forward to the final eschatological rest.' [44] The purpose of God is not yet realised as the New Testament makes clear. The eternal Sabbath rest of God lies still in the future and the observance of the one-day-of-rest-in-seven principle of the Fourth Commandment is not only binding but full of meaning and the hope of a final rest and a better world. In the words of Peter, 'we, according to His promise, look for new heavens and a new earth in which righteousness dwells' (2 Peter 3:13).

Eschatology

As we examine the New Testament scriptures, it is clear that 'eschatology' is to be defined in terms of the first coming of Christ as well as His second coming. The New Testament teaches what is often termed an *inaugurated*, already *realised* eschatology, to be *consummated* at Christ's return. 'The shift from the seventh to the first day reflects the present eschatological situation of the church; the change of day is an index of eschatology already realised, of the new creation rest inaugurated by Christ, especially at his resurrection. Correlatively, the continuation of a weekly rest day

43 J. V. Fesko (2007), *Last Things First*, pp. 190–191.
44 Geerhardus Vos (1996), *Biblical Theology*, p. 141.

is a sign of eschatology still future, a pointer to the eschatological rest to come at Christ's return.'[45]

This sense of the 'already now' and 'not yet' with regard to eschatology is clear from the New Testament and in particular from the writings of the Apostle Paul. This sense is evident from creation: 'For we know that the whole creation groans and labours with birth pangs together until now' (Romans 8:22). It is also evident from the experience of the child of God: 'Not only that, but we also who have the firstfruits of the Spirit, even we ourselves groan within ourselves, eagerly waiting for the adoption, the redemption of our body' (Romans 8:23). There is the anticipated final rest: 'the earnest expectation of the creation eagerly waits for the revealing of the sons of God' (Romans 8:19).

The Church's direction of travel is towards the final resurrection: 'we who are in this tent groan, being burdened, not because we want to be unclothed, but further clothed, that mortality may be swallowed up by life' (2 Corinthians 5:4). The child of God lives from the perspective of the Holy Spirit—'He who has prepared us for this very thing is God, who also has given us the Spirit as a guarantee' (2 Corinthians 5:5). The new man of the new creation is not yet the man who has entered the consummation of the purposes of God. The Christ in whom we have new life is also the Christ who is the 'firstfruits' (1 Corinthians 15:23) from the dead. Christ, the last Adam, 'became a life-giving spirit' (1 Corinthians 15:45). God will 'give life' to the mortal bodies of believers 'through his Spirit' (Romans 8:11). The new man in Christ will enter the final rest of God at Christ's return—'each one in his own order: Christ the firstfruits, afterward those who are Christ's at His coming' (1 Corinthians 15:23).

Hebrews 4

Hebrews 4 is a key New Testament passage for our understanding of the ongoing validity of the Fourth Commandment and the principle of one-day-of-rest-in-seven based on the Sabbath rest of creation. What

45 Ligon Duncan (2003), *The Westminster Confession in the 21st Century*, Vol. 1, p. 138.

better book to reiterate Sabbath observance than the book of Hebrews, which teaches most clearly how all Old Testament ceremonial worship practices were fulfilled in Christ and therefore repealed. The passage helps our understanding of the Sabbath in the post-resurrection of Jesus era in two ways.

An abiding principle

First, the passage helps to see that the Fourth Commandment and the principle of one-day-of-rest-in-seven still applies for the New Testament. A careful exegesis of the passage is able to show: 'rest' for the Church in Hebrews 3–4 is (1) eschatological, (2) entirely future, (3) called 'Sabbath-resting' and (4) grounded in God's creation. The writer quotes extensively from Psalm 95 in chapter 3:7-11 and again repeatedly in chapter 4. 'Using an analogy from covenant history based on Psalm 95:7–11, he compares the present situation of the Church (between the ascension and return of Christ, the high priest in heaven) with Israel in the wilderness, between Egypt/slavery (3:16) and Canaan/rest (4:8).'[46]

The fulfilment of God's promised rest had been provided by Jesus Christ. Those who believe in the Lord Jesus Christ have begun to participate in its reality, but they will participate in the fullness of eternal rest only if they persevere (3:6). Like Israel in the wilderness, they were pilgrims. They were to press on to the heavenly, eternal rest provided by the Lord Jesus Christ'.[47] The final eschatological rest is in the future—*'There remains therefore a rest for the people of God'* (4:9). 'The word used here for "rest" is unique in the New Testament. Consistent with the Septuagint (the ancient Greek translation of the Old Testament), it ought to be translated "sabbath keeping"—"so then there remains a sabbath-keeping for the people of God." We must persevere in our Christian profession, which includes Sabbath-keeping as a fruit of our new life and our rest in Christ, if we are to enjoy that final and eternal rest that Jesus has secured.'[48]

46 Ligon Duncan (2003), *The Westminster Confession in the 21st Century*, Vol. 1, p. 133
47 Joseph Pipa JR (2018), *The Lord's Day*, p. 113.
48 Andrew Clarke (2007), *Love Rules—The Ten Commandments in the 21st Century*, p. 48.

A new day

Secondly, a careful examination of Hebrews 4 also establishes the day of the Sabbath observance. The key verses are verses 9 and 10 and the relationship between them in a study of the passage. Verse 10 gives the grounds and explanation for verse 9. There remains a Sabbath-keeping (4:9) for (because) the one who has entered His rest has himself also rested from his works as God did from His (4:10). There is a change of pronoun in verse 10. The use of the singular pronoun here (instead of the plural in 4:1, 4:3, and 4:11) suggests someone other than the people of God, an individual, has entered his rest as God entered his. This can only refer to the Lord Jesus Christ.

In verse 10, therefore, the writer compares Christ's rest from His work of redemption with God's rest from the work of creation. 'After the Rest-giver had accomplished His work, the New Testament Church kept its Sabbath on the day He entered into His rest, signifying that although we wait for the consummation, we already have begun to participate in this rest.'[49]

The parallel

'This understanding provides a parallel between the work of creation and the work of redemption. At the conclusion of creation, God rested on the seventh day to declare his work completed, to delight in that work, and to promise the eternal rest promised to Adam in the Covenant of Works. When Adam broke the covenant, God renewed the offer of eternal rest through a Redeemer. The seventh-day Sabbath looked forward to that rest. God the Son rested from His work of redemption on the first day of the week as a sign that His work had objectively been accomplished and nothing remained to be done. In the resurrection He entered into the joy of His work and confirmed that eternal life had been purchased (Isaiah 35:10; Hebrews 12:2). By His example, the day was changed.'[50]

---

49 Joseph Pipa JR (2018), *The Lord's Day*, p. 123.
50 Joseph Pipa JR (2018), *The Lord's Day*, p. 120.

The distraction

We must not be distracted by references in the Pauline writings which may suggest, on first reading, to state that the New Testament Church is no longer obligated to observe as a special day. These references are found in passages such as Romans 14:5, Galatians 4:10 and Colossians 2:16–17. The opponents of Sabbath-keeping maintain that the New Testament Church is no longer obligated to observe a special day, with some going so far as to say that to keep the Sabbath on the first day of the week is a form of Judaising. The claim is that 'Sabbath-keeping robs one of Christian liberty.'[51]

The distinction made by theologians and the Reformers that the Word of God contains three types of laws is helpful in this case. There are *moral* laws, *civil* laws, and *ceremonial* laws. The *ceremonial* laws have been fulfilled in Christ; the sacrifices no longer need to be made. The *civil* laws of Israel are not binding on people and nations today. But the *moral* law has not been done away with. It is still in force and binding on everyone.

It is wrong to suggest that, in fulfilling the Law, the Lord Jesus has brought about a sphere of existence where the Law does not apply to the New Testament Church. He denies that it was His intention to abrogate and terminate the Law: 'Do not think that I came to destroy the law or the Prophets. I did not come to destroy but to fulfil' (Matthew 5:17). He states that it is His intention, instead, to fulfil the Law. 'Undoubtedly that involved validating and confirming the Law, but more is conveyed by "fulfil" than the static maintenance of existing standards as they had always been. There is progression and consummation. Jesus brought the Law forward to its full intent and proper expression. He did not disparage it. He ensured that it came to perfect realisation.'[52]

The passages referred to in the previous paragraph address the Sabbath system instituted at Sinai and its typological function in Israel (week, year, and Jubilee year, as well as day), a system which has ceased with the finished work of Christ. The 'progression and consummation' of the Law brought about by the Lord Jesus means that we have certainly left behind

---

51 Joseph Pipa JR (2018), *The Lord's Day*, p. 95.

52 John L. Mackay (2004), *The Moral Law—Its Place in Scripture and its Relevance Today*, p. 41.

the ceremonial laws of the Old Testament, and the typology associated with the observance days associated with feasts and festival. But the 'progression and consummation' means that the Law shines now in all the brilliance of the will of God and in the person of Christ including the shining of His majesty and glory on the resurrection morning, the Lord's Day, that makes the observance of the first day of the week as the weekly Sabbath a great joy as well as a great duty.

Conclusion

We have shown the significance, and the abiding and binding relevance, of the Fourth Commandment in the Old Testament by placing it in the context of protology, eschatology, and soteriology, and God's relationship with humankind. We have also done so by highlighting the significance of the Fourth Commandment within the moral law, as a creation ordinance, and as a covenant sign.

We proceeded to note the continuity between the Old Testament and the New Testament in the biblical teaching of the significance and binding relevance of the Fourth Commandment regarding a new creation, a new man, a new covenant, and the hope of a new heavens and a new earth. We paid close attention to the development regarding the observance of the first day of the week as the Christian Sabbath in the New Testament Church after the resurrection of the Lord Jesus.

The teaching of the New Testament is clear. The Lord Jesus rubber-stamped the first day of the week as the Christian Sabbath to be observed by the Church as the one-day-of-rest-in-seven, a day when the Church was to gather to worship Him, to hear the Word of God, and to spend the time contemplating and rejoicing in, not their own weekly endeavours, but the finished work of their Saviour as the last Adam who has entered into His rest and who waits for the day when He will welcome His Church into the eternal rest of the glory of God.

We must view the Sabbath as a glorious addition to our lives and not a subtraction. We must see it as it is: a gift from God through which we offer ourselves in God in worship, hear what God has to speak into our lives, and be empowered by the sense of the divine power which

God has promised in the careful observance of it. In the words of Old Testament scholar Walter Brueggemann, the Fourth Commandment is the 'crucial bridge that connects the Ten Commandments together. The Fourth Commandment looks back to the first three commandments and the God who rests (Exodus 20:3–7). At the same time, the Sabbath commandment looks forward to the last six commandments that concern the neighbour (vv. 12–17); they provide for rest alongside the neighbour. Sabbath becomes a decisive, concrete, visible way opting for and aligning with the God of rest.'[53]

The life of the Church and the Christian community, and the life of the broken world around us, is crying out for us all to walk in this 'bridge' and to align ourselves with the God of rest. We owe it to our God in worship and adoration and behaviour. We owe it to ourselves, and to the world around us, so that our lives are regulated by God, His Law, and the gospel as we struggle with issues of injustices, identity, discrimination, morality and spirituality.

53 Brueggemann, W (2017), *Sabbath as Resistance*, 10.

Chapter 5: A Day to Worship

Rev. Alasdair J. Macleod

Rev. Alasdair J. Macleod is the former minister of the Knock & Point congregation of the Free Church of Scotland (Continuing)

'I was in the Spirit on the Lord's day...' (Revelation 1:10)

What is the Lord's Day positively for? Why is one day to be set apart from the rest? The answer, of course, is worship. In the Old Testament, the Sabbath was defined positively as a day for worship. Psalm 92 is titled 'A Psalm or Song for the sabbath day', and it constitutes a summons to worship: 'It is a good thing to give thanks unto the LORD, and to sing praises unto thy name, O most High' (Psalm 92:1). Furthermore, worship was specifically anticipated upon the Sabbath from the people of God: 'And it shall come to pass, that from one new moon to another, and from one sabbath to another, shall all flesh come to worship before me, saith the LORD' (Isaiah 66:23). While there were daily acts of ceremonial worship connected with the temple in Old Testament times, there were specific acts related to the Sabbath day (Numbers 28:9–10). Such worship was defined by Christ as a form of work, but such work as was proper and right to be done upon the Sabbath: 'Or have ye not read in the law, how that on the sabbath days the priests in the temple profane the sabbath, and are blameless?' (Matthew 12:5). But the Sabbath, even in Old Testament times, was a day for the Word: 'For Moses of old time hath in every city them that preach him, being read in the synagogues every sabbath day' (Acts 15:21). Christ Himself approved this practice by His own conduct in reading and preaching the Word on the Sabbath (Luke 4:16–30).

Therefore, we should expect that the Lord's Day, as the New Testament Sabbath, should be set apart as a day for worship, and this is exactly what we find in Scripture. This chapter will examine the six key texts that refer to the Lord's Day in the New Testament, to prove that this day is a day for worship. The chapter will then draw evidence from church history that the day has been set apart for Christian worship ever since apostolic times. Finally, it will close with some practical consideration of what a day of worship will look like.

1. The Lord's Day in the New Testament

There are six references to the observance of the Lord's Day in the New Testament, and we shall consider each in turn.

(a) The first Lord's Day

The first of these references concerns the actual day of the resurrection itself:

> Then the same day at evening, being the first day of the week, when the doors were shut where the disciples were assembled for fear of the Jews, came Jesus and stood in the midst, and saith unto them, Peace be unto you. And when he had so said, he shewed unto them his hands and his side. Then were the disciples glad, when they saw the Lord. Then said Jesus to them again, Peace be unto you: as my Father hath sent me, even so send I you. And when he had said this, he breathed on them, and saith unto them, Receive ye the Holy Ghost: Whose soever sins ye remit, they are remitted unto them; and whose soever sins ye retain, they are retained (John 20:19–23).

As the commentator A. W. Pink writes regarding this passage:

> Observe in the first place how the Holy Spirit here emphasises the fact that what follows is a first-day scene. On this first Christian Sabbath the disciples were assembled in separation from the world, and from this point on to the end of the New Testament the first day of the week is stamped with this characteristic: Sunday, not Saturday, was henceforth to be the day set apart for rest from the work and concerns of the world, and for occupation with the things of God.[54]

54 A. W. Pink, *Exposition of the Gospel of John* (Electronic Edition), on John 20:19.

Here we find the disciples of Christ, gathered together, fearful of their enemies, but compelled to be together by the extraordinary, wonderful, almost unbelievable news that they had heard from the women. The body of Jesus could not be found: He was not there, for He had risen. Fear and wonder combined to drive them together. We can well imagine what was in their discussion as they gathered. The promise of Christ that He would rise again, a promise that had bewildered them at the time, now apparently a reality! The Scriptures of the Old Testament, which before had been so veiled in their understanding, were now beginning to open in the light of all they had seen. And the awesome hope of what this meant for them: was this indeed the redemption of Israel?

Here then were the core elements of worship: the believers gathered; the Lord and His salvation their focus of attention; the Word their means of understanding. And what is the result? Christ Himself appears in the midst of the gathering! What a stamp of approval upon the gathered worship of the Lord's Day! And yet it is no more than what the Lord Jesus Himself had promised: 'For where two or three are gathered together in my name, there am I in the midst of them' (Matthew 18:20).

This passage is therefore a profound encouragement to join in gathered worship on the Lord's Day. The same elements of worship are to be found in a faithful and Bible-believing church, and the same promise holds good. Christ will not come physically in His resurrected body as He did here—that coming again is reserved to the Last Day (Matthew 24:30), but He will be present by His Spirit: 'Howbeit when he, the Spirit of truth, is come, he will guide you into all truth: for he shall not speak of himself; but whatsoever he shall hear, that shall he speak: and he will shew you things to come' (John 16:13). Intriguingly, it is actually better that Christ be absent physically from us, for the blessings of His presence by the Holy Spirit are even more beneficial for us: 'Nevertheless I tell you the truth; It is expedient for you that I go away: for if I go not away, the Comforter will not come unto you; but if I depart, I will send him unto you' (John 16:7). The word translated 'expedient' is *sumpherei*, literally 'bearing together', used here in the sense of contributing positive benefit.

The specific benefits of Christ's presence on this first Lord's Day were the assurance that He conveyed to His true believing people: 'Peace be unto you'; the revelation of His atoning work: 'he shewed unto them his hands and his side'; the comfort that they thus received, 'Then were the disciples glad, when they saw the Lord'; the practical direction that He gave them: 'as my Father hath sent me, even so send I you'; and, finally, the gracious spiritual help He conveyed to them: 'he breathed on them, and saith unto them, Receive ye the Holy Ghost: Whose soever sins ye remit, they are remitted unto them; and whose soever sins ye retain, they are retained.' These benefits continue in the gathered worship of the Lord's Day to the present.

As the great Puritan commentator Matthew Henry observed:

> There are three secondary ordinances (as I may call them) instituted by our Lord Jesus, to continue in his Church, for the support of it, and for the due administration of the principal ordinances—the word, sacraments, and prayer; these are, the Lord's day, solemn assemblies, and standing ministry. The mind of Christ concerning each of these is plainly intimated to us in these verses; of the first two, here, in the circumstances of this appearance, the other John 20:21. Christ's kingdom was to be set up among men, immediately upon his resurrection; and accordingly we find the very day he arose, though but a day of small things, yet graced with those solemnities which should help to keep up a face of religion throughout all the ages of the Church.[55]

(b) The second Lord's Day

The second reference to the Lord's Day in the New Testament follows in the same chapter:

> And after eight days again his disciples were within, and Thomas with them: then came Jesus, the doors being shut, and stood in the midst, and said, Peace be unto you. Then saith he to Thomas, Reach hither thy finger, and

55 Matthew Henry, *An Exposition, with Practical Observations, of The Gospel According to St John* (Electronic Edition), on John 20:19.

> behold my hands; and reach hither thy hand, and thrust it into my side: and be not faithless, but believing. And Thomas answered and said unto him, My Lord and my God. Jesus saith unto him, Thomas, because thou hast seen me, thou hast believed: blessed are they that have not seen, and yet have believed (John 20:26–29).

Note that the Jewish method of counting days was to count a portion of a day as one, hence three days in the grave took Christ from 'Friday' afternoon to 'Sunday' morning, and 'eight days' marked the elapse of exactly one week. Therefore, crucially, we see the first day of the week again observed, both by the disciples and Christ. They found it proper, right from the tiny and fragile beginning of the New Testament Church, to gather on the Lord's Day. One week after Christ had risen, His disciples gathered together again. Why? Who was the focus of their thoughts and conversation? Surely, here was a gathering for worship. Here again appeared the risen Christ in the midst, setting His seal upon the appropriateness of this gathering, and again pronouncing His blessing upon it, 'Peace be unto you.' Matthew Henry noted that Christ left one week between these appearances for good reason: 'That he might put an honour upon the first day of the week, and give a plain intimation of his will, that it should be observed in his Church as the Christian sabbath, the weekly day of holy rest and holy convocations.'[56]

There is a further aspect of worship evident here: the correction of false doctrine and restoration of the backslider. Thomas was a true believer, but he lacked faith to believe that Christ was risen indeed. Confronted with the risen, living Christ, the wounds that had purchased His redemption, and the gentle rebuke, 'Be not faithless, but believing', his response was one of adoration: 'My Lord and my God.' Thomas engaged in worship; Christ responded with His assurance, and with a further pronouncement of blessing upon the wider Christian Church: 'Thomas, because thou hast seen me, thou hast believed: blessed are they that have not seen, and yet have believed.'

---

56 Henry, *Exposition of John* (Electronic Edition), on John 20:26.

Here then is the pattern for the worship of the first day of the week, established and approved by the Head of the Church, and its benefits made evident.

(c) Pentecost

The next 'first day' of which we have record is the Jewish ceremony of Pentecost, recounted in Acts 2. This occurred, as the law specified (Leviticus 23:15–16), fifty days after the day after the Sabbath of Passover week. Counting as the Jews did, a part of a day as a day, this therefore occurred exactly seven weeks after the resurrection of Christ. Remarkably, Christ's resurrection occurred on the very day when the sheaf of the firstfruits of harvest was waved before the Lord. What significance there is in that! 'But now is Christ risen from the dead, and become the firstfruits of them that slept' (1 Corinthians 15:20). We should not be surprised at the awesome harmony of the Scriptures, and yet we are!

Seven weeks later, the first day of the week, the Lord's Day, was the day chosen for the fulfilment of prophecy in the outpouring of the Holy Spirit in power upon the New Testament Church. The American theologian Robert Dabney underlined the significance of Pentecost occurring on the Lord's Day:

> This epoch was indeed the creation of a new world in the spiritual sense. The work was equal in glory and everlasting moment to that first creation which caused 'the morning stars to sing together and all the sons of God to shout for joy'. Well might God substitute the first day for the seventh when the first day had now become the sign of two separate events, the rising of Christ and the founding of the new dispensation, either of which is as momentous and blessed to us as the world's foundation.[57]

Furthermore, the seal of the outpouring of the Holy Spirit follows upon the proper use of the Lord's Day—as a day of worship. Reading Acts 2:1 in the light of Acts 1:14, we see that the disciples were 'all with one accord in

---

57 Robert L. Dabney, *Discussions*, C. R. Vaughan, ed., (Richmond, Va., 1890), i, p.532.

one place' on the Lord's Day, where 'one accord' can only mean that they were gathered together, on the Lord's Day, to continue 'with one accord in prayer and supplication'. The Lord's Day was from the very beginning a day for gathered worship and earnest prayer for the young Church, and, under the leading of the Holy Spirit, for the bold and fearless preaching of the gospel (Acts 2:14–41).

As Dabney concludes:

> At this all-important stage every step, every act, of the divine providence recorded by inspiration in the Acts was formative and fundamental. Hence we must believe that this event was meant by God as a forcible precedent, establishing the Lord's day as our Christian Sabbath.[58]

(d) The Lord's Day for public worship

One of the most telling descriptions of the worship of the Apostolic Church comes in Acts 20, when Paul and his companions were at Troas: 'And upon the first day of the week, when the disciples came together to break bread, Paul preached unto them, ready to depart on the morrow; and continued his speech until midnight' (Act 20:7). Here we see the first day of the week established as the day of public worship: it was the day the disciples gathered; it was the day for the preaching of the Word at length and for the sacrament of the Lord's Supper to be observed; and it was a day reserved from travel for gathered fellowship and worship with the Lord's people. All the positive aspects of Sabbath observance are here evident in the New Testament Church's observance of the Lord's Day.

As the eminent Canadian minister William Matheson wrote in his thoughtful discussion of the Sabbath: 'The primary obligation, therefore, resting upon Christians under the Fourth Commandment is the gathering of themselves together unto the Name of the Lord for his public worship.'[59] If the Apostolic Church is our model, then here is the pattern to be followed.

---

58 Ibid., p. 532.

59 William Matheson, *May Sabbath-Keeping Prevent Church-Going?* (n.p., 1936), p. 46.

(e) The Lord's Day for collections

Further confirmation of the status of the first day of the week as the day of gathered worship in the Apostolic Church is found in a passing reference in Paul's first epistle to the church at Corinth: 'Upon the first day of the week let every one of you lay by him in store, as God hath prospered him, that there be no gatherings when I come' (1 Corinthians 16:2). Here we see again the first day taken for granted as being a day for the church to gather together, by implication for public worship in general, and specifically for one particular element of worship, charitable giving to the Lord's cause. Here is a mandate for the present-day Church to continue to observe the Lord's Day with all of the essential elements of public worship, including financial collections.

(f) The Lord's Day for private worship

The final Scriptural reference to the Lord's Day is very significant, as it shows this day being observed by a believer even when separated by persecution from the rest of the Church, the Apostle John on Patmos: 'I was in the Spirit on the Lord's day…' (Revelation 1:10). Here we see the day of the week being adequately identified by a name that has obviously entered standard usage in the Christian Church; John knew his readers would need him to give no more explanation about which day he meant. Then we see that day identified specifically with Christ, 'the Lord's' day, using the same word in the original language (*kyriakos*) that is used to identify 'the *Lord's* supper' in 1 Corinthians 11:20. This day is Christ's day: it commemorates his resurrection, but it is also the day of which He is Lord: 'Therefore the Son of man is Lord also of the sabbath' (Mark 2:28). This day has significance and is observed even apart from the wider Church: John sets apart that day to be 'in the Spirit', which can only be a reference to the exercise of private worship. Probably it indicated reading the written Word and meditating upon it, 'The sword of the Spirit, which is the word of God' (Ephesians 6:17), and prayer, 'Praying always with all prayer and supplication in the Spirit, and watching thereunto with all perseverance and supplication for all saints' (Ephesians 6:18).

What a seal God set upon this time of private devotion! On this day John was granted the revelation that would comprise the final book of the Bible. What visions he saw that day! What warnings to the churches! What wonders for the redeemed! What horrors for the wicked! What glory for Christ! The Revelation sets an implicit mandate of Divine approval upon the observance of the Lord's Day as a day of private as well as public devotions, a day to be observed to the end by the Church of Christ.

2. The Lord's Day in church history

The consistent testimony of the whole of church history is that the first day of the week has been observed as the Christian day of worship. The early manual of Christian teaching called the *Didache*, likely dating to the first century AD, commands: 'But every Lord's day gather yourselves together, and break bread, and give thanksgiving after having confessed your transgressions, that your sacrifice may be pure.'[60] The early church father Ignatius (died c. 108) wrote in his epistle to the Magnesians that Christian believers are 'no longer observing the Sabbath, but living in the observance of the Lord's Day'.[61]

Justin Martyr (c. 100–c. 165) wrote in his First Apology a description of Christian worship on the Lord's Day in the second century:

> And on the day called Sunday, all who live in cities or in the country gather together to one place, and the memoirs of the apostles or the writings of the prophets are read, as long as time permits; then, when the reader has ceased, the president verbally instructs, and exhorts to the imitation of these good things.... But Sunday is the day on which we all hold our common assembly, because it is the first day on which God, having wrought a change in the darkness and matter, made the world; and Jesus Christ our Saviour on the same day rose from the dead.[62]

60 *Didache*, ch. 14, accessed online at URL: http://www.earlychristianwritings.com/text/didache-roberts.html

61 Ignatius to the Magnesians, ch. ix, accessed online at URL: http://www.earlychristianwritings.com/text/ignatius-magnesians-roberts.html

62 Justin Martyr, *First Apology*, ch. 67, accessed online at URL: https://www.newadvent.org/fathers/0126.htm

Similarly, Tertullian (c. 155–c. 240), an important early Christian theologian, urges that the Lord's Day be kept as a day of rest from other business, for the purpose of worship:

> We, however (just as we have received), only on the day of the Lord's Resurrection ought to guard not only against kneeling, but every posture and office of solicitude; deferring even our businesses lest we give any place to the devil.[63]

Another early Church father, Cyprian (c. 200–258), offers a thoughtful argument, drawing from the typology of the Old Testament, to suggest that the Lord's Day should really be considered the *eighth* day of the week! It should be considered the beginning of a new week after the end of the old. This allowed him to draw a striking parallel with the Jewish practice of circumcision, which was done on the eighth day of the child's newborn life:

> For in respect of the observance of the eighth day in the Jewish circumcision of the flesh, a sacrament was given beforehand in shadow and in usage; but when Christ came, it was fulfilled in truth. For because the eighth day, that is, the first day after the Sabbath, was to be that on which the Lord should rise again, and should quicken us, and give us circumcision of the spirit, the eighth day, that is, the first day after the Sabbath, and the Lord's day, went before in the figure; which figure ceased when by and by the truth came, and spiritual circumcision was given to us.[64]

Cyprian's language is convoluted and difficult, but his meaning is that Christ rose again on the first day of the new week, beginning the new risen and eternal life, which all His people shall enjoy in Him. This is like circumcision, done at the start of a new week of life, symbolising a new beginning with sin removed (signified by cutting off the foreskin of

---

63 Tertullian, *De Oratione*, 23, accessed online at URL: http://www.tertullian.org/anf/anf03/anf03-51.htm

64 Cyprian, *Letter LVIII*, para. 4, accessed online at URL: https://www.ccel.org/ccel/schaff/anf05.iv.iv.lviii.html

the child). We are summoned to the real thing, not to the symbolic act of circumcision, but a spiritual circumcision, which is the renewal of life in Christ. As the Apostle wrote to the Christian believers in Colosse: 'If ye then be risen with Christ, seek those things which are above, where Christ sitteth on the right hand of God' (Colossians 3:1). In our observance of the Lord's Day, we therefore remember not only Christ's resurrection, but the significance of that resurrection for us His people.

A significant development in the history of the Church occurred after the Emperor Constantine had converted to Christianity. He issued a decree in 321 setting aside the first day of the week as a day of rest in the Roman Empire, a change presumably intended to benefit the Christian Church.[65] This would suggest not only that the Lord's Day was already being observed as the Christian day of worship, which we know from the many sources cited above, but that Christians desired to keep it as a day of rest free from unnecessary secular work. It suggests that by 321 there was a widespread understanding in the Christian Church that the obligation of the Fourth Commandment now referred to the Lord's Day, and a desire therefore to abstain from secular work upon it.

Athanasius (c. 296–373), a church father of this period, wrote with great clarity on the Old Testament Sabbath as replaced by the Lord's Day:

> The Sabbath was the end of the first creation, the Lord's day was the beginning of the second, in which he renewed and restored the old in the same way as he prescribed that they should formerly observe the Sabbath as a memorial of the end of the first things, so we honour the *Lord's day* as being the memorial of the new creation.[66]

Similar clarity is found in his contemporary, Eusebius of Caesarea, in a commentary he wrote on the ninety-second Psalm, which is titled 'A psalm or song for the Sabbath day':

---

65 Philip Schaff, *History of the Christian Church* (New York, 1891), iii, pp. 379–380.

66 Athanasius, *On Sabbath and Circumcision*, 3, accessed online at URL: http://www.sabbaths.org/meeting.html [Note however that the attribution of this work to Athanasius has been questioned; it may be by another early church writer].

> The Word [Christ] by the new covenant translated and transferred the feast of the Sabbath to the morning light, and gave us the symbol of the true rest, the saving Lord's day, the first of light, in which the Saviour gained the victory over death. On this day, which is the first of the Light and the true Sun, we assemble after the interval of six days, and celebrate holy and spiritual Sabbath; even all nations redeemed by him throughout the world assemble, and do those things according to the spiritual law which were decreed for the priests to do on the Sabbath. All things which it was duty to do on the Sabbath, these we have transferred to the Lord's day, as more appropriately belonging unto it, because it has the precedence, and is first in rank, and more honourable than the Jewish Sabbath. It hath been enjoined on us that we should meet together on this day, and it is evidence that we should do these things announced in this psalm.[67]

Other evidence of a Sabbath rest upon the Lord's Day can be found in the early Celtic Church of Scotland and Ireland, where strict Sabbatarianism seems to have prevailed from the earliest days of the Church. A former Church History Professor of the Free Church of Scotland, Donald Maclean, published a valuable treatise establishing this point.[68] He points out that Patrick and Columba can both be shown to have observed the Lord's Day, and that a surviving Gaelic manuscript, its content dating no later than the beginning of the ninth century, the *Cáin Domnaig* ('Law of the Lord's Day'), mandates a strict observance, including 'the prohibition of baking, washing, shaving, fetching of fuel and other forms of labour, on the Lord's day'.[69]

In 789, Charlemagne (742–814), the King of the Franks, and later the first Holy Roman Emperor, decreed that all ordinary work was forbidden on the Lord's Day as a breach of the Fourth Commandment.[70] Thereafter, the Church was theoretically Sabbatarian in its practice, albeit with much variety in strictness of practice. Scotland seems to have declined in this regard as the Middle Ages progressed: Queen Margaret (c. 1045–1093)

67 Quoted in Dabney, *Discussions*, i, pp. 537–538.
68 Donald Maclean, *The Law of the Lord's Day in the Celtic Church* (Edinburgh, 1926).
69 Ibid., v–vi, cf. pp. 39–43.
70 Ibid., p. 28.

complained of the irreverence of the Scottish clergy in the observance of the Lord's day as Sabbath, 'devoting themselves to every worldly business on it just as they did on other days'. Similarly, evidence would suggest that Sabbath-breaking became widespread in other European countries until the dawn of the Reformation.[71]

Protestantism was associated with a recovery of a high view of the Lord's Day. Martin Luther (1483–1546) wrote in condemnation of 'He who without special need works and transacts business on the Lord's day' and added that this commandment particularly forbids 'slothfulness and indifference to worship'.[72]

John Calvin (1509–64), in his *Institutes of the Christian Religion*, did not argue for a strict observance of the Lord's Day in the manner of the Old Testament Sabbath, but did apply the Fourth Commandment as requiring 'that all may observe the legitimate order appointed by the Church, for the hearing of the Word, the administration of the sacrament, and public prayer.'[73]

Similarly the *Heidelberg Catechism* (1563) of the Reformed Church in Germany interpreted the Fourth Commandment as declaring God's will 'that, especially on the festive day of rest, I diligently attend the assembly of God's people'.[74]

Equally, the Dutch Synod of Dort taught that the Fourth Commandment is 'Moral in fact, because the fixed and enduring day of the worship of God is appointed, for as much rest as is necessary for the worship of God and holy meditation of him.'[75]

But the observance of the Lord's Day as Sabbath found its clearest and fullest statement in the documents of the Westminster Assembly of Divines, and especially in the Larger Catechism:

71 Ibid., pp. 54–58.

72 Martin Luther, *Works of Martin Luther with Introductions and Notes* (Philadelphia, Pa., 1916), ii, p. 360.

73 John Calvin, *Institutes of the Christian Religion* (Edinburgh, 1845), i, pp. 465–466.

74 Heidelberg Catechism, q.103, accessed online at URL: https://www.crcna.org/welcome/beliefs/confessions/heidelberg-catechism

75 Synod of Dort, Session 164, accessed online at URL: https://rscottclark.org/2012/08/the-synod-of-dort-on-sabbath-observance/

> Q117: How is the sabbath or the Lord's day to be sanctified?
>
> A117: The sabbath or Lord's day is to be sanctified by an holy resting all the day, not only from such works as are at all times sinful, but even from such worldly employments and recreations as are on other days lawful; and making it our delight to spend the whole time (except so much of it as is to be taken up in works of necessity and mercy) in the public and private exercises of God's worship: and, to that end, we are to prepare our hearts, and with such foresight, diligence, and moderation, to dispose and seasonably dispatch our worldly business, that we may be the more free and fit for the duties of that day.[76]

This answer expresses the settled view of the English Puritans and the Scottish Covenanters, that is, the view of arguably the ablest and most spiritually-minded theologians the British Isles have ever produced, that the Lord's Day is the Christian Sabbath Day in its obligations both of holy rest and of positive worship from the believer, both private and public.

3. The Lord's Day today

The Lord's Day is to be observed as a day of worship in the present age. It is a busy day, of positive activity, full of benefit for man, but for the soul rather than the body, for eternity rather than for time. The key aspects of this observance are as follows.

(a) Public worship

First, and of primary importance, is the gathering together with the Lord's people for the public worship of God. This has been shown already to be at the heart of the New Testament descriptions of the observation of the Lord's Day. A Sabbath wilfully spent apart from the fellowship of God's people in gathered worship is a Sabbath profaned, whatever private activities are engaged in. 'LORD, I have loved the habitation of

76 Westminster Larger Catechism, Q.117, accessed online at URL: https://www.fpchurch.org.uk/about-us/important-documents/the-larger-catechism-1648/

thy house, and the place where thine honour dwelleth' (Psalm 26:8). The physical gathering together is essential unless necessary circumstances in the Lord's will prevent that personal attendance. The promises associated with public worship refer specifically to physical gathering: 'For where two or three are gathered together in my name, there am I in the midst of them' (Matthew 18:20).

The gathered worship must centre upon the glory and enjoyment of God Himself. The Puritan Thomas Brooks wrote:

> It is the duty and glory of a Christian to rejoice in the Lord every day, but especially on the Lord's day. God reserves the best wine, the best comforts, and the choicest discoveries of himself, and of his love, and of his Christ, and of his glory for that day, and all to make his people 'joyful in the house of prayer' (Isaiah 56:7). [...] To fast on the Lord's day, saith Ignatius, is to kill Christ; but to rejoice in the Lord this day, and to rejoice in all the duties of this day, and to rejoice in that redemption that was wrought for us on this day, this is to crown Christ, this is to lift up Christ.[77]

But this worship is itself beneficial to man: says Matthew Henry, 'The Sabbath is a market-day, a harvest-day for the soul; it is an opportunity; it is time fitted for the doing of that which cannot be done at all, or not so well done at another time.'[78]

Therefore the Fourth Commandment requires of believers attendance at church; focused and attentive participation; heartfelt singing of the Psalms; earnest appeal to the Lord in the heart as we join in prayer; and a humble and teachable spirit under the Word, read and preached. Let us, says Thomas Watson, 'have our ears chained to the Word'.[79] When we do so, then we shall find that 'The sabbath was made for man' (Mark 2:27).

---

77 Thomas Brooks, 'London's Lamentations of the Late Fiery Visitation,' in *The Works of Thomas Brooks* (Edinburgh, 1861–67), vi, p. 299.

78 Matthew Henry, 'A Serious Address to those that profane the Lord's Day,' in *The Complete Works of the Rev. Matthew Henry* (Edinburgh, 1853), i, p. 132.

79 Thomas Watson, *The Ten Commandments* (Edinburgh, 1965), p. 112.

(b) Private worship

But public worship will only benefit, when it comes in the context of a wider life of private devotion. A well-spent Sabbath begins with God, with time spent reading the Word and praying. 'But thou, when thou prayest, enter into thy closet, and when thou hast shut thy door, pray to thy Father which is in secret; and thy Father which seeth in secret shall reward thee openly' (Matthew 6:6). The Sabbath worship commended in Psalm 92 is specifically 'To shew forth thy lovingkindness in the morning, and thy faithfulness every night' (Psalm 92:2). In the private context, this means to declare His greatness in attributes and works to ourselves, and so to bring forth worship from our own hearts: 'Rejoice in the LORD, ye righteous; and give thanks at the remembrance of his holiness' (Psalm 97:12).

Private worship continues in the family circle. Our responsibility is to declare His praise to our children, and so to instruct and disciple them in the truth. All true believers must share the determination of Joshua: 'but as for me and my house, we will serve the LORD' (Joshua 24:15). This nothing more than obedience to the command: 'And, ye fathers, provoke not your children to wrath: but bring them up in the nurture and admonition of the Lord' (Ephesians 6:4). And God is pleased to remember His covenant, His family relationship, with His people, and so works in families: 'Turn, O backsliding children, saith the LORD; for I am married unto you: and I will take you one of a city, and two of a family, and I will bring you to Zion' (Jeremiah 3:14). How often is the promise to the Philippian jailer's family overlooked: 'Believe on the Lord Jesus Christ, and thou shalt be saved, and thy house' (Acts 16:31).

Family worship, therefore, is vitally important. It is a duty every day for the godly parent; the instruction in the Word goes alongside normal secular life (Deuteronomy 6:6–7). But especially on the Lord's Day, there is uninterrupted time for worship in the family circle, and this itself is an observation of the Fourth Commandment in practice. The description of family worship in Psalm 118 is followed just a few verses later by celebration of 'the day': 'The voice of rejoicing and salvation is in the tabernacles [or homes] of the righteous: the right hand of the LORD doeth valiantly.... This is the day which the LORD hath made; we will rejoice and be glad in it' (Psalm 118:15,24).

It may be objected that 'the day' in that context refers to the day of Christ, that is, to the New Testament age, though many sound commentators have understood it to refer to the Sabbath.[80] But even if we take that interpretation, then we have all the more reason surely to adore Christ for His coming and work on the identified 'Lord's Day' of New Testament Scripture. If this now, this age, is the day of Christ, then let us be sure that 'the voice of rejoicing and salvation' is in our homes every day, and, above all, on the Lord's Day.

In the continuation, and especially at the close of the Lord's Day, how appropriate to bring to Him then what we have seen of His greatness, and to thank Him for all He is to us. Let the day end as it has begun, in heart-devotion to the Master. Considered experimentally, we can well appreciate and likely identify with the truth of Thomas Watson's well-known description of the benefit of the Sabbath:

> When the falling dust of the world has clogged the wheels of our affections, that they can scarce move towards God, the Sabbath comes, and oil the wheels of our affections and they move swiftly on. God has appointed the Sabbath for this end. On this day the thoughts rise to heaven, the tongue speaks of God, and is as the pen of a ready writer, the eyes drop tears, and the soul burns in love. The heart, which all the week was frozen, on the Sabbath melts with the word. The Sabbath is a friend to religion: it files off the rust of our graces; it is a spiritual jubilee, wherein the soul is set to converse with its Maker.[81]

What a benefit is a well-kept Sabbath!

> For thou, Lord, by thy mighty works
> hast made my heart right glad;

80 e.g., Matthew Henry, *An Exposition, with Practical Observations, of The Book of Psalms* (Electronic Edition), on Psalm 118:24.
81 Watson, *Ten Commandments*, pp. 94–95.

And I will triumph in the works
  which by thine hands were made.

How great, Lord, are thy works!
  each thought of thine a deep it is:
A brutish man it knoweth not;
  fools understand not this

(Psalm 92:4–6).

Chapter 6: A Day to Hope

Rev. Iain Smith

Rev. Iain Smith is the retired minister of the Harris congregation of the Free Church of Scotland (Continuing)

There remaineth therefore a rest to the people of God (Hebrews 4:9).

The Sabbath as anticipation of Heaven, a foretaste of blessing.

Introduction

As a subject of Christian doctrine, the biblical Sabbath is an extensive theme to study. That is reflected, to some extent, by the topics listed in this publication. The title for this particular section, *A Day to Hope*, suggests a future dimension to the Sabbath day. Expounding this dimension of God's holy day should surely avoid the typical controversies usually associated with the biblical teaching on the Sabbath, its relevance, and its proper observation.

However, an agreement among Christians on this feature of the Sabbath is by no means universal throughout the Church. Religious subjects lacking definitive biblical teaching and clarity are bound to result in various views and interpretations. The basic reference text in this particular instance is Hebrews 4:9, which reads 'There remaineth therefore a rest to the people of God' (KJV). A sub-heading has also been provided: 'The Sabbath as anticipation of Heaven, a foretaste of blessing.'

There are many excellent writings in current usage on the biblical Sabbath and on the Lord's Day. The Lord's Day Observance Society have published many articles on the Sabbath over the years. Among the best of the more substantial works produced by others is *The Lord's Day* by Joseph A. Pipa. There is also the more extensive work by Francis Nigel

Lee, entitled *The Covenantal Sabbath*. These sources, and many others, cover every aspect associated with God's holy day.

Not too many of the available writings have ventured into a detailed exposition of the future dimension of the Sabbath, as related to our reference text, other than to make broad references to a heavenly rest. Indeed, some commentators are almost reluctant to accept that there is a deliberate alluding to an eternal rest in the Hebrews 4:9 text. John Owen, by way of example, does not speculate on this at all in his commentary on the Hebrews passage.

Perhaps it is not surprising that there is little written on the eternal aspect of the believer's rest. In terms of revelation, there is not a whole lot to go on when exploring the great eternity as the everlasting abode of the saints. Further, there is limited value in the symbols and imagery recorded in the apocalyptic writings of Scripture. Also, our minds are unused to functioning in areas beyond the parameters of time and space. However, there is sufficient information to help us in forming a broad, if somewhat blurred, vision of the Paradise above.

This chapter will be structured on relevant aspects of the biblical Sabbath and Lord's Day. It will explore some issues which may not have an overtly obvious application to the heavenly rest of God's saints. The chapter will begin by exploring the idea of a divinely-ordained *rest* presented to us at various stages of inspired revelation. The intention is to demonstrate how God ran a linear redemptive thread through four major stages of this *rest* in providence and in history. It is this thread that has always provided Christian people with the hope of an everlasting rest with Jesus, who is Lord of the Sabbath. These four stages are: (1) the Genesis rest undertaken by God; (2) the Canaan rest of the children of Israel; (3) the believer's rest in Jesus Christ, and (4) the everlasting rest of the saints.

Prior to dealing with these topics, we should acknowledge the inclusion of Sabbath Day keeping in God's moral and religious code, which we know as the Ten Commandments. Although there is no direct reference in the first nine chapters of Genesis subsequent to the initial Sabbath, until the time of the Flood, nevertheless, we do believe that the Seventh Day Commandment continued, as viable and binding as its nine counterparts, from Eden to Sinai. Furthermore, the Sabbath was also understood as both holy and a day of rest.

That early expectation of rest from the hand of God may be indicated by Lamech's choice of name for his son Noah (which means rest). Also regarding Noah's practice aboard the ark, his understanding of a weekly sabbath seems to be reflected in the seven-day cycles mentioned in Genesis 8:10 and 12. This view of the perpetuity of the Sabbath from the beginning is further confirmed by Moses when, at the beginning of their wilderness journey, prior to the giving of the Law, he spoke in this way: 'This is that which the LORD hath said, Tomorrow is the rest of the holy sabbath unto the LORD: bake that which ye will bake today, and seethe that ye will seethe; and that which remaineth over lay up for you to be kept until the morning' (Exodus 16:23). The rest and the holiness of the Sabbath were so significant to the wellbeing of the people that repeated references to the Fourth Commandment can be found in Exodus 20, Exodus 31, Exodus 35, Leviticus 23, and Deuteronomy 5.

Charles Hodge suggests two important reasons underlining why God established the Sabbath as a holy day of rest. These were to make His people think about things unseen and eternal and that as a day of rest the Sabbath pointed them to the eternal rest spoken of in Scripture.[82] John Murray speaks of the threefold redemptive focus of the Sabbath as the Lord's Day in New Testament times. These are the past where the focus is on the Lord's resurrection, the present where resurrection joy benefits believers, and the future where it points to the inheritance of the saints.[83] These references are highlighted in this chapter simply to provide some background to the proposed pattern of our heavenly rest symbolised in the areas to follow.

The Genesis rest undertaken by God

'And on the seventh day God ended his work which he had made; and he rested on the seventh day from all his work which he had made' (Genesis 2:2). This text should be read along with Isaiah 40:28, part of

82 Charles Hodge, *Systematic Theology*, Vol. 3, p. 322.
83 John Murray, *Works*, Vol. 1, p. 224.

which reads, 'the everlasting God, the LORD, the Creator of the ends of the earth, fainteth not, neither is weary; there is no searching of his understanding.'

Every serious reader of Scripture knows that Genesis 2:2 is not to be understood in the usual sense of the term *rest*. As the Isaiah passage reminds us, the eternal God is of omnipotent power and thereby is inexhaustible. Nevertheless, the context of Hebrews 4:9 indicates an association between God's *rest* at the culmination of His creative activity and the ongoing *rest* offered on the Sabbath. It is also worth noting that the terms *rest* and *sabbath* share the same root source in biblical usage. Evidently, God has embedded the rest which He offers to humanity in general and to believers in particular, within the concept of His own declared rest.

Of course, God's rest is not one of inactivity. As Calvin points out in his comment on this verse: '...as God sustains the world by his power, governs it by his providence, cherishes and even propagates all creatures, he is constantly at work.'[84] However, God's rest was defined by the cessation of His creative industry. Hence our rest, in its physical sense, is to be acquired, in part at least, by a cessation of what we normally do on other days of the week.

The juxtaposition of God's rest in the Hebrews passage and the rest promised to believers indicates to us that there was a messianic element even to the first Sabbath rest. This would become more apparent as history and providence developed under God's guiding hand.

We should also note, with the commentator Barnes, that the word translated in Hebrews 4:9 as rest, is the Greek word *sabbatismos*. This is different from the word *sabbaton*, usually translated as the sabbath. In fact, this form of the noun, *sabbatismos*, is used nowhere else in the New Testament. According to Barnes, a literal translation would be a keeping sabbath. And, of course, this keeping sabbath reflects the character of the day God declared as hallowed and sanctified.

It is important at this stage to link all this information with the fact that the first Sabbath was not verified in similar fashion to the other six

84 John Calvin, *Commentary on Genesis 2:2*.

days of the creation week. These days are defined for us in the following manner: the evening and the morning were the first day; the evening and the morning were the second day, etc. This formula is not stated regarding the seventh day. It simply says, on the seventh day God ended His work and rested on the seventh day from all His work.

So, the first Sabbath in human history was deliberately left open-ended by God, indicating an ongoing dimension and application. It seems, therefore, that in its highest meaning the first Sabbath, and every Sabbath thereafter, looked forward in hope of an infinitely greater rest than any twenty-four-hour period could afford us.

We can end this section by quoting Barnes again. Referring to the sabbath [*sabbaton*], he states that this word 'denotes the time—the day, the keeping, or observance of it; the festival.' Whereas, referring to the keeping sabbath [the *sabbatismos* of Hebrews 4:9] Barnes declares that it means 'a resting, or an observance of sacred repose and refers undoubtedly to heaven, as a place of eternal rest with God.'

Those that within the house of God are planted by his grace, They shall grow up, and flourish all in our God's holy place (Psalm 92:13).

The Canaan rest of the children of Israel

It would not be accurate to suggest that nothing existed with regard to a messianic Sabbath rest in the thought and language of people in the lead-up to Canaan. When God gives people hope, that hope never dies. Whatever the poet Alexander Pope meant by his often-quoted words, hope springs eternal, there is much truth to these words in Christian philosophy.

There is every reason to believe that God's promise of a Messiah (the seed of the woman) gave birth to a living hope of divine rest that sin could not eliminate. We have already seen evidence of this with the generation of Noah's parents. It was their hope of divine messianic rest that led them to name their son, Noah. Then the famous ark associated with Noah, wherein the remnant rested during the judgement of the Flood, became a link in the chain that would lead to the promised rest yet to be more fully realised.

Biblical authors recognised this thread or chain of divine hope. Moses was the first to speak of Canaan as a place of rest. He taught the children of Israel: 'For ye are not as yet come to the rest and to the inheritance, which the LORD your God giveth you' (Deuteronomy 12:9). There was obviously hope and expectation of some form of rest when the Israelites would cross over Jordan. However, many of the adults disqualified themselves from any claim on that rest. The psalmist picks up on that by recording these solemn words, 'Unto whom I sware in my wrath that they should not enter into my rest' (Psalm 95:11).

In the context of our reference text in Hebrews 4:9, the Canaan rest provides the backdrop to the psalmist's condemnatory words quoted in Hebrews 4:3. Verse 1 of Hebrews 4 sets the theme by alluding to Canaan. Then the narrative immediately focuses on the prospect of rest for New Testament believers through the preaching of the gospel. That is followed by a warning of disqualification, along with an allusion to the Genesis Sabbath rest (v. 3). The Genesis rest is again referred to in verse 4, with the disqualification repeated in verse 5. The wilderness conduct of the Israelites is highlighted in verse 7. Then a confirmation that the Canaan rest was mere typology, pointing to the hope of rest yet to come (v. 8). So, in these verses, including our reference text, we have a clear link between God's rest following creation, the Canaan rest for the children of Israel, the rest provided in the gospel for New Testament believers, and then an indication of eternal rest.

Therefore, the open-ended *sabbatismos* of Genesis continued conveying its hope of rest throughout the epochs of history, whilst constantly reaching out to the next phase of the everlasting repose beyond the scenes of time which God had promised at the dawn of history.

He said, I'll give Canaan's land
for heritage to you;
While they were strangers there, and few
in number very few.

(Psalm 105:11–12)

The believer's rest in Jesus Christ

It was with great relief and expectation that the promised Messiah eventually arrived on earth. It is without parallel in human history that a promise given before writing began should remain vital millennia later. Through angelic messages, the dreams of men and women, an army of prophets and poets, God kept the hope of messianic rest alive. Almost as amazing is the reality of believers that never gave up on that promise, generation after generation, century after century. This is well illustrated by Simeon who waited in the temple at Jerusalem for the one he called 'the consolation of Israel' (Luke 2:25).

There were many indications and prophecies on what awaited Messiah in the course of securing rest for His people. David and Isaiah stand out in the details they recorded regarding this matter (Psalm 22 and Isaiah 53). However, a startling illustration of what awaited Messiah in His redemptive quest to perfect what was necessary to secure this rest, appeared much earlier in history.

Appropriately it took place with the man whose name predicted the rest Messiah would offer to the heirs of eternal salvation, Noah. It appeared in what the world calls the rainbow. Only it is not called a rainbow in Scripture, but simply a bow—as in bow and arrow: 'I do set my bow in the cloud, and it shall be for a token of a covenant between me and the earth' (Genesis 9:13).

The symbolism is quite profound. The bow is a token of both the wrath and mercy of God. A token of wrath in that the world should always associate the rainbow with the destruction of the ancient world on account of God considering that the wickedness of man was great in the earth, and that every imagination of the thoughts of his heart was only evil continually (Genesis 6:5). But the bow was also a token of mercy in that God promised that, when He would look upon the bow, He would remember the everlasting covenant between Him and every living creature of all flesh that is upon the earth (Genesis 9:16).

The symbolism of this bow can be taken a further two steps, both of which are relevant to the redemptive mission of Messiah in securing rest for the children of God. The first step is in following the line of the bow.

It begins, as it were, on the earth, then arks up to heaven, then comes back down to earth again. In other words, it is set amid sinful humanity, it reaches up to a holy and just God, then it comes back down to a sinful earth. It is not unlike Jacob's ladder, regarding which we are told that it also was first set on earth and then reached up to heaven (Genesis 28:12).

Then the final step to the symbolism of the bow relates to the question: if there is a bow, then where is the suggested arrow? We can justifiably respond by suggesting that the arrow exists where it would otherwise be, in the apex of the bow and pointing, as it were, to God in heaven. Only God is an invisible target for the arrow, and He cannot be slain. But He has to be slain if His people are to enjoy an eternal sabbath rest.

Therefore, God would do what He did later on Mount Moriah in type—He provided for Himself a Lamb (Genesis 22:8). So, to become the target for this arrow, God's Son said, 'Sacrifice and offering thou wouldest not, but a body hast thou prepared me' (Psalm 40:6, interpreted by the apostle in Hebrews 10:5).

And in the fullness of time the incarnation of God's Son materialised and eventually the arrow found its target at Calvary Golgotha. Without detailing the horrors of that experience, suffice it to say that the full force of divine wrath against sin fell on Jesus, invading His consciousness whilst the arrow of perfect justice penetrated His very soul. However, out of that terrible storm came a calm—the eternal rest for the saints of God had been achieved.

This is beautifully expressed by the metrical version of Psalm 107:30:

> Then are they glad, because at rest
> and quiet now they be:
> So to the haven he them brings,
> which they desired to see.

Yet, the beginning of the story concerning Jesus of Nazareth did not seem promising concerning any hope of eternal messianic rest. He was, in the eyes of men, a poor boy born into a humble home in a despised corner of Palestine. And, despite some phenomena surrounding His conception in the virgin's womb and eventual birth, He showed little indication of being a link in the chain leading to heavenly rest for the elect of God. This was not helped by Him, the Messiah-in-waiting, living under the radar, as He did for the first thirty years of His life.

Nevertheless, the day dawned when all that changed. The transformation in the life of Jesus of Nazareth from being a carpenter to the Messiah who would offer rest for Jews and Gentiles began, appropriately enough, at the approximate spot where another Jesus (Joshua) led the children of Israel over the river Jordan and into the Canaan rest.

At his baptism Jesus was confirmed in His Messianic role by the appearance of the Triune God at the riverside, Father, Son, and Holy Spirit. Following which, during His ministry, Jesus famously issued one of the most gracious invitations ever heard on earth, and it was rest-centred. In Matthew 11:28–30 it reads like this: 'Come unto me, all ye that labour and are heavy laden, and I will give you rest.'

It is a pity that the words of Jesus in this invitation are often read to the exclusion of verses 29–30 of the same chapter. It is these next verses that more fully explain the nature of this rest. Jesus continued by saying: 'Take my yoke upon you, and learn of me; for I am meek and lowly in heart: and ye shall find rest unto your souls. For my yoke is easy, and my burden is light.'

This is not the rest typically associated with the weekly Sabbath rest. There is a rest from one's weekly toil. But there is also a spiritual rest from trying to justify ourselves before God with our good works and much else besides. We are to leave aside all that makes us labour under a heavy burden in this respect and surrender to the claims of Jesus Christ by living under the yoke of His Word and finished work on the cross of Calvary.

It is surely worth quoting John Gill regarding this. He insists that it is 'spiritual rest here, peace of conscience, ease of mind, tranquillity of soul, through an application of pardoning grace, a view of free justification by the righteousness of Christ, and full atonement of sin by his sacrifice; and eternal rest hereafter...'[85] That last comment indicates that even this rest

85 John Gill, *Commentary on Matthew 11:28–30.*

in the Messiah and His finished work is not an exhaustive interpretation of God's open-ended *sabbatismos* rest. There is more yet to come.

> O why art thou cast down, my soul?
> Why, thus with grief opprest,
> Art thou disquieted in me?
> in God still hope and rest.

The everlasting rest of the saints

'There remaineth therefore a rest to the people of God.' We can see now that the trajectory of God's sabbath rest is one that takes us, in hope, ever onwards and ever upwards. It is a rest that yearns for the complete fulfilment of that open-ended sabbath upon which the sun will never set. Let the believer's faith be great or small; this is every Christian's shared inheritance in Jesus Christ.

The intended destination is heaven, the abode of the everlasting God, the throne-room of King Jesus, the holy environment of angels, the long-home of God's people, the place of perfect blessedness and happiness, the only created environment where sin and uncleanness are barred from entry. Further, believers arrive at this destination in style. Those destined to enter its holy portals before the second coming of Christ will be heralded in under angelic protection (Luke 16:22).

Yet, there are difficulties in probing this heavenly environment from the perspective of sinful eyes, deceitful hearts, corrupt minds, and stubborn wills. We can speculate based on biblical imagery, helped by the creative artistic endeavours of sincere Christian writers and artists. But we are left then struggling to make sense of pictures such as a physical throne, streets of gold, a lamb, trees, and a river, etc., etc. This type of imagery is not, of course, to be taken literally. But without that imagery, where do we go? Much has been written on the imagery presented in the Revelation of John. But it is mostly all the speculation of men, some of which can make sense and some of which is wild imagination.

One option is to explore the only other holy sinless environment presented to us in Scripture. Here at least we are on safe ground. There is a warrant to do this based on the close association which Scripture makes between the Paradise of Eden and the Paradise above. In John's vision in Patmos a connection between those two locations was intended by, for example, the appearance of the tree of life in Genesis 2 and in Revelation 2 and 22. So, we shall seek some insight into our eternal sabbath rest by considering some details recorded concerning the first Paradise.

Eden

Our inability to imagine what heaven is actually like can be frustrating. Exacerbating our vexation is the fact that heaven is not merely a spiritual entity, an invisible realm where spiritual beings happily repose. There is also a physical dimension to heaven in that there are physical beings present, such as Enoch, Elijah, and the Lord Jesus, albeit in glorified bodies. Yet, despite the biblical imagery designed to help, we are quite incapable of creating meaningful pictures of that glorious Paradise. It is simply too other-worldly for our sin-laden imaginations.

However, we do have a faint glimpse of heaven in the holy environment of the first Paradise, the Garden of Eden. Like heaven, this also was a sinless and perfect location. But even here we find ourselves struggling. How can we imagine anything or anyone in this world that was perfect and beautiful, without spot, wrinkle, or blemish? We cannot even fully grasp what God meant when He saw regarding His finished work that 'behold, it was very good' (Genesis 1:31). We are even incapable of imagining what the sinless and perfectly holy Jesus was actually like as a Man, in terms of His physical and earthly existence.

Yet, unlike any other species, humanity has been created with the ability to appreciate the striking beauty of colours, contours, and objects, sometimes with breath-taking wonder. But all the beauty and wonder we now see is tinged with the dual pollution of sinful matter and our corrupt imaginations.

A further challenge regarding appreciation of the first Paradise is in the question of what distinguished it from an otherwise perfect and flawless world? Why did God have to create a garden distinct from His already beautiful world?

One discernible reason was to make our first covenant parents even more aware of God's nearness and presence in their lives. The tree of life was a sacramental emblem of God's presence on earth. Amongst Jewish and Christian commentators there has been much speculation over this tree and its fruit. Turretin dismisses any suggestion that the tree of life held the key to immortality by whatever fruit it bore. He argues that the tree of life was a symbol of the divine presence, reminding Adam that the source of his present and future life was in God.[86]

Turretin also states that Adam understood that his present happy life would eventually evolve into a heavenly life should he continue obedient and upright. He further suggests that the tree of life was a type of Christ, who bestows this life on His people. This, he argues, is what is meant by the references to the tree of life in Revelation 2:7 and 22:2. All of which makes the original Paradise rather special.

That focus on God's presence in Eden fits in with the glimpse given to us of heaven in Revelation 7 where we read of the heavenly congregation focused on the divine presence (v.9), 'a great multitude, which no man could number, of all nations, and kindreds, and people, and tongues, stood before the throne, and before the Lamb...' These saints of God knew who it was that sat upon the throne: 'Salvation to our God which sitteth upon the throne, and unto the Lamb' (v. 10).

This perpetual worship in heaven forms part of the saints' rest in glory. Hence John was to record this testimony for our benefit: 'And I heard a voice from heaven saying unto me, Write, Blessed are the dead which die in the Lord from henceforth: Yea, saith the Spirit, that they may rest from their labours...' (Revelation 14:13).

Another aspect of Eden which may help us to understand the environment awaiting us in our eternal sabbath rest, is the purity and innocence which characterised Adam and Eve at that stage of their lives. What were they like, physically and mentally, and spiritually, as God *put* (or placed) them in Paradise on that first Sabbath? We can also speculate on this regarding Jesus. But this we do know: He was perfect, without spot

86 Turretin, *Vol. 1*, pp. 580–11.

or blemish. In body, mind, heart, soul, thoughts, and imagination, Jesus was purer than the driven snow.

But then so were Adam and Eve before they sinned against God. Apart from Jesus, Adam and Eve were the two most beautiful people that ever lived. They had been created a mirror-image of God in His communicable attributes. In knowledge, righteousness and holiness, they echoed the character of God perfectly. In their sinlessness, innocence and love they were a carbon copy of who the Man Jesus of Nazareth would be in the fullness of time.

Their superior mental and intellectual agility can be seen in Adam's ability to name the animals according to their nature. Spiritually their conscience was at perfect peace without the least embarrassment at their own nakedness. And they were in flawless unison with the mind of God. They saw Him everywhere. They would have had a constant awareness of His presence and required no appointment for prayer, worship and fellowship. Surely this must be the very essence of being at rest! So, there in Eden, we can easily imagine the reality of beauty, perfection, harmony and holiness, as well as the peace of heaven.

Heaven

This must be what life is like in the Paradise above for those enjoying their never-ending rest in Christ, only magnified a thousandfold. Physically they are in glorified bodies—a concept way beyond the capacity of our minds to grasp. We have faint glimpses of the resurrected and glorified body in the experience of the Lord Jesus. He was capable of extraordinary things such as appearing in a room with the doors closed (John 20:19). When He appeared from heaven to the Apostle Paul, it was as a light brighter than the noonday sun (Acts 22:6).

Intellectually, the saints at rest in Paradise understand the ways of God infinitely better than the ablest of them did in this world. Further, whilst remaining finite, all the sinful limitations of their minds have been removed through the culmination and perfection of their sanctification. Being finite, they will continue learning eternally about the character of God, the sheer wonder of their Saviour, and the gracious role of the Holy

Spirit in their lives. Spiritually, they are enjoying a calibre of communion and fellowship which we can scarcely imagine or even dream about.

All this and so much more is implied in the teaching of the Shorter Catechism on the subject of the believer's death. Question 37 asks: 'What benefits do believers receive from Christ at death?' Part of the answer is that 'the souls of believers are at their death made perfect in holiness and do immediately pass into glory.'

It was Jesus, more than any other, who named that glory with a title that resonates with people in all civil cultures throughout the world. In John 14 it reads as the Father's house of many mansions. It invites an almost domestic view of our heavenly home.

In any case, this transformation from time to eternity will be an introduction to our keeping sabbath, our *sabbatismos* rest that shall never end. A faint glimmer of this could be had by taking the Sabbath on earth, when best observed, and extending the idea to eternity, and removing every shred of imperfection from its observance.

Certainly, there are numerous parallels between the ideal of a Sabbath on earth and the eternal Sabbath in heaven. The Sabbath is holy; so is heaven. It is set aside for worship; so is heaven. It is for the contemplation of God; so is heaven. It is a day for believers to call a delight; so is heaven. It is a day of rest from daily toil, worldly cares, and earthly anxieties. Heaven is where all of these concerns will be set aside forever. John Owen says that God is pleased to fill us and exercise us all to prepare us duly for eternal rest with Himself.

Therefore, the weekly Sabbath should be loved and appreciated for many reasons, not least, in its symbolism of our eternal rest. Past generations of Christians were possibly more likely to think along such lines. In places where the Christian Church was strong and where the Sabbath was historically observed carefully in homes, this may have lent itself to more focused heavenly thoughts on this subject. The communal quietness of the Sabbath, family attendance at the local church, homes where worldly pursuits were discouraged and the reading of good books was the practice, it was almost natural to see how the Lord's Day pointed to the environment of heaven.

What better way to conclude this chapter than with a quotation from Matthew Henry who has summed up this entire theme of the promised rest for God's people in his own succinct but profound style.

> From the certainty of another rest besides that seventh day of rest instituted and observed both before and after the fall, and besides that typical Canaan-rest which most of the Jews fell short of by unbelief; for the Psalmist has spoken of another day and another rest, whence it is evident that there is a more spiritual and excellent sabbath remaining for the people of God than that into which Joshua led the Jews (vv. 6–9), and this rest remaining, [1] A rest of grace, and comfort, and holiness, in the gospel state. This is the rest wherewith the Lord Jesus, our Joshua, causes weary souls and awakened consciences to rest, and this is the refreshing. [2] A rest in glory, the everlasting sabbatism of heaven, which is the repose and perfection of nature and grace too, where the people of God shall enjoy the end of their faith and the object of all their desires. [3] This is further proved from the glorious forerunners who have actually taken possession of this rest—God and Christ. It is certain that God, after the creating of the world in six days, entered into his rest; and it is certain that Christ, when he had finished the work of our redemption, entered into his rest; and these were not only examples, but earnests, that believers shall enter into their rest: *He that hath entered into rest hath also ceased from his own works as God did from his.*[87]

For God of Zion hath made choice;
there he desires to dwell.
This is my rest, here still I'll stay;
for I do like it well.

(Psalm 132:13–14)

Thou wilt me show the path of life:
of joys there is full store
Before thy face; at thy right hand
are pleasures evermore.

(Psalm 16:11)

87 Matthew Henry Commentary on Hebrews 4:9.

Chapter 7: Conclusion

Rev. Andrew W.F. Coghill

Rev. Andrew W.F. Coghill is the minister of the Scalpay congregation of the Free Church of Scotland

The opening chapter of this book began with the statement 'In the history of the human race, there has never been a week without a Sabbath.' Each succeeding chapter has likewise built upon the undeniable truth that the God of eternity, who chose to create time itself, hard-wired the Sabbath into His divine plan: 'Therefore the Son of man is Lord also of the sabbath' (Mark 2:28).

Potential readers of this book will most likely fall into one of three categories. The smallest category is likely to be those who are unbelievers and who may pick up this book only to scoff at its contents; and if they do read it, they will do so (initially at least) only to be better informed as to the arguments they want to oppose. Whilst naturally the authors would hope and pray for the conversion of all such, it should at least be acknowledged by such opponents that the foregoing chapters represent not a quaint and obscure *aberration* of Christianity, but a soundly argued presentation of *what the Bible actually teaches* in both Old and New Testaments in relation to the Sabbath. The 'opposition' then of these would-be readers is not so much against the 'Sabbatarian' expression of Christianity, but to *Christianity per se*, in *any* form of public expression. Such opponents will probably say that they *are* not anti-Christian, but what they mean is that people are free to be Christian as long as it is kept so private, personal and secret that nobody else should be exposed to its teachings. Such a demand leaves the Christian with a stark choice—to obey the world and be silent, or to obey the Lord who commanded His disciples to 'Go ye into all the world, and preach the gospel to every creature' (Mark 16:15). Whilst some might say that upholding the Sabbath is not the same as preaching the gospel, it is undeniably the case that the sanctifying of the day *bears witness* to the God who created (and sanctified) it.

The second and middle category of potential readers (though in terms of our readership probably a segment almost as small as the first) would be Christians who would not regard the Sabbath as any part of what they would see as *their* 'New Testament' Christianity, beyond the bare fact of going to church. One of the tragedies of the Christian Church is that *this* group would comprise the overwhelming majority of the professing church in the twenty-first century. There are many reasons for this, but perhaps the biggest single factor has been that since the late nineteenth century western Christianity has become increasingly man-centred as opposed to Christ-centred. The twin-pronged attack of Darwinism and German Higher Criticism shook the faith of many in the Church, causing a crisis of confidence in the authority and reliability of God's Word. For some, the only way to survive was to accommodate themselves to the tastes of the world; and the world's demand was that everything be 'optional'.

One by one the Ten Commandments were dispensed with, but those areas of the country where Bible-believing Christianity remained strong—such as the Highlands and Islands of Scotland, some parts of Northern Ireland, and some pockets within the Welsh valleys—kept the faith as a whole. Yet the part that everybody *saw* to be *different* from the 'liberal' or unbelieving world was the way that Bible-believing Christians observed the Sabbath. Whole communities fell silent once a week, save for the voices raised in worship.

Scratch the surface and one would find that these communities would also be amongst the most law-abiding and domestically stable in terms of family life (Commandments five and seven), could leave their doors unlocked at night or in their absence (Commandments eight and ten), would abhor lying and profane language (Commandments nine and three), would have a disproportionately high ratio of those going into nursing and the caring professions, so valuing human life from the womb to its natural end (Commandment six) and would worship in unadorned churches free of what is so often euphemistically termed 'Christian artwork' (Commandment two). As Bible-believing Christians they declined to put their own preferences before those of God (Commandment one), so when it came to the First Day of the week, they recognised it to be *His* Day rather than theirs (Commandment four), albeit made *for* them.

This does not make the Sabbath a quaint or culture-bound hostage of these communities any more than are the commandments to abstain from adultery or murder, or to have no other gods before the Lord. It merely means that where the Christian faith was taken solemnly and seriously, it was taken as a whole, rather than treating some parts as optional extras.

We are all to an extent the product of our upbringing and experience, and there is a natural reluctance in man, and perhaps particularly in the church, to accept or acknowledge that we may have been getting it wrong all these years. The tendency is to assume that if something was against the Law of God, then surely the church, or more specifically '*my* church', would never acquiesce in it. If it *does*, then whatever is acquiesced in must surely be OK. That is the natural man's default position. But if we *are* to consider the possibility of being wrong, then the liberal 'Christian' will justifiably turn upon his Reformed brother and say, 'Well? Do you accept that *you* may have been wrong in promoting the Sabbath all these years?'

Christians are by definition followers of Christ, so for any answer we can only go to Christ. What does He say? Aside from the statement that 'Therefore the Son of man is Lord also of the sabbath'—and it is hard to imagine Christ delighting in lordship over something which He intended to discard as being of no consequence—He also says, 'Search the scriptures; for in them ye think ye have eternal life: and they are they which testify of me' (John 5:39). A little further on, He prays for His disciples, 'Sanctify them through thy truth: thy word is truth' (John 17:17). If nothing else, this book has endeavoured to give a comprehensive exposition of what the duly searched-out *Scriptures*, God's Word which is truth, *say* about the importance of the Sabbath, and the One who is the Lord of the Sabbath. It makes no appeal to cultural identities or to any perceived heyday of Hebridean spirituality.

The Church of Jesus Christ desperately needs to re-engage with its King and Head. Too much of the Church has been drifting for a century and a half, downplaying the claims of Christ and His Word upon the human soul and human behaviour in the world, even for those who are not *of* the world. This has infected *every* part of the Church's life and witness. The Sabbath is by no means the *only* aspect of faithfulness to God with which we need to re-engage, but it *is* the glue that holds all the other aspects of such faithfulness together. Re-examining our attitudes to the Sabbath will compel us to re-examine every other aspect of the outworking of our faith.

The present writer began his spiritual journey with very laid back attitudes towards the Lord's Day—once church was over and done with, it was 'my day' rather than the Lord's, to do what I wanted, like an extra Saturday. I know only too well that the idolatry of self says, 'God wants me to happy, and that means doing what I want to do.' This is no more than a cheerful way of expressing the doleful conclusion to the Book of Judges: 'In those days there was no king in Israel: every man did that which was right in his own eyes.' The chapters of that book illustrate amply the bitter fruit of going our own way rather than God's. Only gradually, from an initial defiance, and then grudging defensiveness, and then returning again to the Word of God, and then looking at what kind of witness and example was set by *not* following that Word, as opposed to following it, so gradually did my own grudging compliance give way step by step to a far deeper love for the Lord and for His Day. I can truthfully say that the more I love the Lord, the more I love His Day and want to honour Him in it. Far from being the quaint and old-fashioned preserve of a few isolated communities, the Christian Sabbath is a core element of the Christian gospel. The idea that to reach the world we must first reflect *its* values rather than God's has been weighed in the balance and found wanting. It was the revival of evangelical Christianity in the late eighteenth and early nineteenth centuries that produced organisations like the Trinitarian Bible Society and the Lord's Day Observance Society. These were neither Highland nor Hebridean, nor Scottish nor Presbyterian in origin. They were originally the work of devout London-based Anglicans at a time when London was the capital of a world empire; and within a year the founding father of the Lord's Day Observance Society became the Anglican Bishop of Calcutta in India from where, on the same principles of Biblical Christianity, he founded schools and colleges that now span three different countries (India, Bangladesh and Myanmar). The Sabbath, especially now in its New Testament manifestation of the Lord's Day, was 'made for man', for the *whole* of humanity, not just for one country or culture. It is a gift to all mankind, and it is especially incumbent upon the Lord's own people to honour their own Lord, upon His own Day.

The third and final category of this book's readership will be the smallest portion of the population as a whole but paradoxically the largest likely group of our actual readers. These are the people who love the Lord's Day because they love the Lord. As a young married couple each learn more and more about the different ways and preferences of their beloved, and so adjust their own lives and practices each to accommodate the other, so the Bride of Christ gradually delights to conform her ways and practices more and more to honour her Lord, and His Day, and to delight in the new freedoms it gives her, the rest that she is able to enjoy, the freedom to worship and to lay aside with a clear conscience the shrill demands of the world which insist upon monopolising our attention and energies '24/7'. The Christian who loves the Lord will, for their part, insist that the most 'the world' can be allowed to have of them is 24/6 (and even that is not a healthy proportion!). By the grace of God 'The Sabbath was made for man,' and it was the Lord of the Sabbath who made it for us.

It is the hope of the authors that such believers will be strengthened and empowered by the contents of this book. For those believers will themselves undoubtedly have endured not only the sneering contempt of an unbelieving world but sadly also the 'superior' scolding of more 'liberal' professing Christians who will paint them as Pharisees and legalists, getting hung up on 'secondary' issues, or what is worse, will claim perhaps that they are placing obstacles in the path of gospel mission and outreach, loving their 'traditions' more than the souls of the lost. It is often claimed that the Sabbath no longer applies to 'New Testament Christians' because it has been 'fulfilled' in Christ. One wonders whether those advocating such abandonment of the Lord's Day would say that a Christian is now 'free' to commit adultery, to steal, to murder, to lie and to covet, to blaspheme the Lord's Name, or to set up and worship graven images, if the Law being 'fulfilled' in Christ means that none of it any longer applies? But as this book has amply demonstrated, the commandment and divine example of Sabbath rest and worship goes much deeper than Mount Sinai and Ten Commandments—it goes all the way back to Creation and applies to all mankind.

If this book helps in any way to bolster the conviction of those who love our Lord and His Day, to reassure brothers and sisters in Christ that they are not strange, not legalists or Pharisees or culture-bound traditionalists, but that the doctrine they love and strive to uphold is rooted and built squarely upon the foundation of the Word of God, the Holy Scriptures of the Old and New Testaments, then the labours of its authors will have been worthwhile. Sabbath observance is not an aberration but a central plank of mainstream Christian orthodoxy, reduced certainly in the level of its present *observance*, but only because the very orthodoxy of mainstream Christianity is itself so diminished at this present time. If we can show to the world what this day means *to us*, then the world will sooner or later want to know *why*, and there on a plate is a gospel opportunity to 'be ready always to give an answer to every man that asketh you a reason of the hope that is in you with meekness and fear: Having a good conscience; that, whereas they speak evil of you, as of evildoers, they may be ashamed that falsely accuse your good conversation in Christ' (1 Peter 3:15–16).

That stone is made head corner-stone,
which builders did despise:
This is the doing of the Lord,
and wondrous in our eyes.

This is the day God made, in it
we'll joy triumphantly.
Save now, I pray thee, Lord; I pray,
send now prosperity.

(Psalm 118:22–25)